visib

D1556658

DEATH AND THE INVISIBLE POWERS

The World of Kongo Belief

SIMON BOCKIE

INDIANA UNIVERSITY PRESS

Bloomington and Indianapolis

© 1993 by Simon Bockie

All rights reserved

The paper used in this publication meets the minimum requirements of
American National Standard for Information Sciences—Permanence
of Paper for Printed Library Materials, ANSI Z39.48-1984.

Manufactured in the United States of America

Library of Congress Cataloging-in-Publication Data

Bockie, Simon, date
    Death and the invisible powers : the world of Kongo belief /
Simon Bockie.
        p.   cm.
    Includes bibliographical references and index.
    ISBN 0-253-31564-6 (alk. paper). — ISBN 0-253-20808-4 (pbk. :
alk. paper)
    1. Kongo (African people)—Religion.   2. Death—Religious
aspects.   3. Ancestor worship—Zaire.   4. Zaire—Religion.   I. Title.
BL2480.B24B63   1993
299'.683931—dc20   92-30614

1 2 3 4 5   97   96   95   94   93

*I dedicate this book to
the Spirits, my daily guardians*

CONTENTS

PREFACE

Until today, the West has done most of the explaining of African existence. The time has come for Africans themselves to set forth their values and identities as only they are capable of doing. We are all aware of the negative terms with which the West has distorted the perception of the African continent, terms that still dominate the popular mind and the news and entertainment media: "dark," "savage," "primitive," a place of suffering, disease, and social chaos. Yet long before Western adventurers came to the Kongo or Central Africans were brought to the New World as slaves, there was a well-organized religious system and social order; life was sustained by a uniquely African spirituality as complex and profound as any in the world. Far from being a place of primitive blankness that has to be filled in by supposedly superior Western values, this region of Africa has its own sources of vitality, sophistication of thought, and spiritual enlightenment.

In spite of the enormous—and destructive—impact of the West, the social fabric of life in the Kongo is still held together by its traditional beliefs and spiritual practices. The Christian churches of the West, which originally came with the purpose of destroying African spiritual culture and replacing it with the European model, have found that native religions are swallowing up Christianity and revising it in the light of their own traditions, a process that has accelerated with political independence. For example: Kimbanguism, a new Christian movement, has sprung up since the 1950s independently of other churches, centering itself on the prophet-martyr Kimbangu, who died in a Belgian prison. Its membership is now perhaps over one million. Kimbanguism draws heavily on Kongo spiritual traditions. Its blessing, calling on "the Father, the Son, and the Holy Spirit," adds a fourth being: "and *tata* [Father] Kimbangu." He has achieved the status of revered ancestor.

The culture of the Kongo people is very much alive and adaptive to change while preserving the integrity of its unique inner life. Africans must continue to reaffirm and base their future development on their own traditional world view. And if the West is willing to listen instead of trying to impose its own values, it can learn much.

I was born in a village in Lower Zaire and participated from the earliest age in the spiritual rites and traditions, both African and European-Christian (as brought by Swedish evangelical missionaries). I went on to the National University of Zaire at Kisangani, where I majored in religious studies and developed a keen interest in tracing and understanding my own cultural roots. That was the beginning of the research that led to this book. Serving as an itinerant preacher, I wandered from village to village in the Manianga sector of Lower Zaire, interviewing elders and other knowledgeable people, who talked with me freely in the Kikongo language we both spoke. Such people are the local "libraries" of knowledge, wisdom, and memory of tradition preserved and handed down orally. I wanted to explore as deeply as I could the inner meaning of the way of life I had shared with them since childhood, to understand it from the inside in a way impossible for missionaries and anthropologists from the West, who unavoidably, and with the best of intentions, feel themselves to be in a superior position. African religions have been examined by the West as exotic objects, often peculiar and incomprehensible or repellent, rather than as valid and meaningful responses to the universal terms of human existence.

I have begun this study with an account of the dynamics of social relationships within the Kongo community. This is necessary in order to understand Kongo spiritual beliefs, which are communal rather than individualistic as in the West. The Kongo spiritual universe can be defined as the community of invisible powers that give order and direction to all of life. In contrast to the Western view, which sets up polarities between God and man, human beings and nature, dominion and subservience, wealth and poverty, Kongo belief stresses equality and community, in a continuum that extends through all existence. From the African point of view, the Western dualities, which pit forces against each other, are essentially an expression of aggressive power that always requires an adversary. The African community always seeks a harmonious return to equilibrium, and its spirituality serves that end. While the West preaches brotherhood to quell disruptive social behavior and is forced to jail those who do not respond, the Kongo community practices a subtle system of incentives and restraints that has developed traditionally over a long period, obviating the need for prisons except in the larger cities, where the Western way of life tends to prevail.

The system of belief that supports the Kongo community has been called "superstitious" and "primitive" by the West. It is probably safe to say that a majority of Europeans and Americans assume that African religions will, in time, be wiped out by the natural triumph of the science and technology, the economy and social forms, of the West, as the indigenous cultures of the Americas and Australia almost have been. That is not likely to happen, however. There has not been a wholesale destruction or absorption of the African peoples, as occurred in the New World and Australia. Africans, like Asians, have survived European colonialism and, in spite of continuing Western domination, are in the process of rebuilding their cultures out of their own traditional beliefs and values. Even if the Kongo people refashion age-old beliefs in a new light, they will remain tenaciously faithful to the spiritual sources that have sustained them for centuries.

The hope embodied in this book is that it will help preserve the knowledge and wisdom of the community for the young people who feel, as I did, the need to return to their roots; that it will inspire African-Americans to realize that they have an important spiritual heritage to draw on for strength and a sense of identity; and that Westerners can learn that there is actually light in the heart of what they have imagined to be darkness.

The immense importance of African spirituality to African-Americans is only beginning to be appreciated. As Albert J. Raboteau states in *Slave Religion,*

> African styles of worship, forms of ritual, systems of belief, and fundamental perspectives have remained vital on this side of the Atlantic, not because they were preserved in a "pure" orthodoxy but because they were transformed. Adaptability, based upon respect for spiritual power wherever it originated, accounted for the openness of African religions to syncretism with other traditions and for the continuity of a distinctive African religious consciousness.[1]

Raboteau also estimates that "a large percentage of American slaves came from West Africa and from the Congo-Angola region,"[2] the region where this study is centered. My own personal experience in America convinces me that many essential characteristics of Kongo culture have survived among African-Americans, even in small and unexpected ways—as when an African-American porter at Kennedy airport called me "brother" on my arrival. Anyone who reads this book will come to realize the meaning of this greeting to me. African-American leaders have recently recognized that establishing a cultural identity is one of the foremost needs of the African-American community, recommending that the term *African-American* replace the term *black*. That would shift the emphasis from color and race to culture and area of origin, paralleling the terms *Asian-American, Native American,* and so on. This raising of cultural consciousness calls for a more intensive understanding of African cultures. And the sustaining life of every culture is its system of spiritual beliefs.

In these pages I have freely drawn on my own experience and that of members of my family, and have recorded the words spoken at rites and ceremonies which I have observed or participated in. I am responsible for all translations into English from Kikongo or French texts. My aim has been to create a picture of Kongo belief as experienced by the people themselves, as human beings confronting a universe of mixed blessings and suffering, especially in the villages where cultural roots lie deepest.

This work is based on a dissertation for my doctoral degree at the Graduate Theological Union in Berkeley, California. I have considerably revised and updated it for the present publication. I owe the initial stimulus for this study to Reverend Bahelele Jacques of Luozi, Bas-Zaire. He was a rich storehouse of information, which he freely shared with me. I wish also to thank the members of my dissertation committee, Professors Albert J. Raboteau, Mark Juergensmeyer, and Elizabeth Colson, who originally advised me to publish this work. I am grateful to my good friend William Drake, Professor Emeritus of the State University of New York, for his constant encouragement in revising the original work and for valuable editorial assistance.

Death and the Invisible Powers

I

THE SPIRITUALITY OF A COMMUNAL PEOPLE

Beginning with Community

European-American spirituality is individualistic: each man or woman is seen in direct personal relationship with a transcendent God. The secular community and the individual spiritual life are separate, sometimes even in conflict, but always with a sense of tension and mutual alienation between the worldly and the unworldly. Churches, religious orders, and communes, or societies of like-minded persons, are formed in order to establish a communal life dominated by spiritual beliefs, rising above and distancing themselves from the secular. Worship is usually confined to designated buildings or meeting places and scheduled times.

This Western outlook must be set aside if one is to penetrate to the heart of Kongo spirituality. For here one finds no separation of the secular and the spiritual, no isolation of the individual and his or her God. The community itself is viewed as the embodiment of spiritual reality, a reality present everywhere, at all times. Each person realizes his or her nature through relationship with others in the community rather than through transcendence. This community furthermore extends through all life to include not only the visible beings but also those who are unseen. To understand Kongo spirituality, then, one must begin with the nature of the Kongo community, the way the Kongo people see and experience their communal life from the inside.

1

The Kongo People

All African peoples have a strong sense of their identity as a group, as a kind of great family occupying a traditional and historic area or region. The Kongo people—or BaKongo, to use the proper plural form—occupy the Central African coast on both sides of the Zaire River, from the Congo Republic on the north, through Zaire into Angola, and extending inland several hundred miles. Their language, Kikongo, is one of the major languages of Zaire and the Congo Republic. The Kingdom of Kongo, flourishing impressively when Europeans first reached Africa, was historically one of the great premodern African civilizations. The present-day BaKongo, though in the midst of rapid social change, still derive their character and their way of life from the enduring traditions of their ancestors.

Such a large and ancient culture is of course subdivided into many localized, though still extensive, communities. My own people are the BaManianga, who occupy an area of several hundred square miles in Lower Zaire, lying mostly north of the Zaire River and spilling into the Congo Republic. The river isolates them, to a considerable extent, from the capital, Kinshasa, and greater Zaire. When Europeans drew national boundaries in Africa, they did so for their own political and economic purposes, disregarding the ethnic identities of the native people, sometimes dividing them between two or three nations while lumping together others traditionally hostile to one another. My study of Kongo spirituality will center on BaManianga, the people whose heritage I know as my own.

The Land of Manianga: Isolation and Rejection

At the outset BaManianga, like other Kongo groups, lived in today's Angola, the birthplace of all BaKongo before migrating northward. According to tradition, the place designated as their capital, Kongo dia Ntotila, was first discovered by a hunter who while chasing a wounded animal let it go in order to contemplate the beauty of the place. Fascinated, he decided to move his family and settle there. He named it Kongo, meaning "a hunting land."[1] This is reflected in the Kongo proverb, "Kongo belongs to a strong hunter; if you are not strong enough, you cannot rule it" (Kongo dia nkongo a ngolo, vo kwena ye ngolo ko, Kongo kuyala dio ko). A weak person can never expect to lead a Kongo group.

Eventually political and religious turmoil caused people to migrate from the Angolan center to settle in regions to the north. Such were the roots, according to tradition, of all Kongo groups we know today.[2]

According to my informants, BaManianga received their name because they settled in a despised area; *Manianga* comes from the Kongo verb *nyanga* (to reject, to give up, to despise). Manianga was portrayed as an abominable land, and the people who chose to dwell there were considered abhorrent in relation to other Kongo groups: rejected because of their headstrong behavior in crossing the Zaire River and going against the judgment of the other groups, who expected no one to do so.[3]

Some, however, do not trace the word into earlier history but believe that it arose at a later date from the name of a big market on the north bank of the Zaire River. This market, which still exists today, was so successful in the mid–nineteenth century that neighboring groups often attended it. When they were asked, "Where are you going or coming from?" their answer was, "We are going to/coming from Manianga market," that is, the market of BaManianga. Stanley recorded that "Manianga was a great market which was very well attended. Slaves, ivory, rubber, oil, pigs, sheep, goats and fowl were sold and bought by people coming from all over the area."[4] The earlier meaning of the word—"despised"—became obscured by the great reputation and success of the market. Not many BaManianga today are aware that before becoming famous for their market they were viewed as abominable.

It would be misleading, however, to say that the greatness of their market completely eradicated their sense of rejection. The area is still isolated from the rest of Zaire. Main roads, railroads, and cities are nonexistent. This isolation, due initially to the presence of the gigantic Zaire River and the people's inability to build bridges across it, continued under Belgian rule. Manianga was the only area in Lower Zaire which did not have a high school during colonization. But because of their thirst for learning, BaManianga since independence have opened high schools in every corner of the area, whether or not they have qualified teachers. Still, the Zaire government shows no sign of encouraging further improvement. When I was at the National University of Zaire, Kisangani, the Manianga students there were planning to raise money to build a highway between Luozi, the administrative center of Manianga, and Kimpese, the center connecting Manianga with other parts of the country. During rainy periods it may take two or three days to reach Kimpese from Luozi, a distance usually traveled in four or five hours. The dusty road turns to thick mud in which a car may be mired for hours or days. But the students' project was stopped by the government for being "tribal." The people today are weary of being ignored, isolated, and condemned to suffering under one regime after another.

Despite the lack of government concern for their physical well-being, BaManianga are one of the more advanced groups in Zaire in other respects, as John M. Janzen writes: "If the region was drastically underdeveloped economically, it could boast of a high degree of literacy among the villagers, and by 1965 one of the highest percentages of university students of any similar area in the Congo."[5] Ironically, after the region had so long been deprived of schools by the Belgians, the first university graduate in the whole country was from Manianga.

BaManianga are scattered throughout the savannah countryside of Manianga *territoire*. As is usually the case when a language has been spoken for centuries by people settled in a given region, their language, Kikongo, varies from one locality to another. Often I had a hard time conversing with old persons from Mongo-Luala. Their nasal accent is unfamiliar to those from other areas.

There are two main seasons: dry from June to October and rainy from November to May. Because the region lies close to the Equator, there are no changes of season from summer to winter as in the temperate zones. Most of the farming and agricultural activities take place in the rainy season. Given their technology, BaManianga may be classified in the category of advanced horticulturists with two major tools: machete for men and hoe for women. They grow maize, eggplant, pumpkin, rice, peanuts, sorghum, beans, peas, yams, manioc, sugar cane, oranges, and other crops. A man wishing to get seriously into the farming business locates his work several miles from the village. He wakes around five in the morning and may walk up to three hours to reach his fields, where he expects a better harvest and can be more devoted to his labor. To farm near the village is less profitable, for when anything goes wrong in the village, he may be the first to be called in or consulted, often at the time he should be completely absorbed by his work. A woman, however, centers most of her agricultural activities near her village.

Gender and Community Structure

The egalitarian principle of power sharing among age groups and genders, along with the competitive struggle over it that characterizes individualistic societies, is absent among BaKongo. Age and sex strictly determine membership in different subgroups within the local community. African societies, and Manianga society in particular, are divided into two separate and distinct worlds: masculine and feminine. Men and women do not live together in the same house even when they are united by marriage. While the husband sleeps in the "big house" *(nzo yayinene),* his wife often sleeps in the "kitchen house" *(kikuku);* while the husband eats at a table in his room, his wife often eats on the floor in hers. There are no scheduled meals at which all family members sit down together. The layout of a typical Manianga village is strongly gender oriented, with important men occupying the front row of dwellings followed by their wives' houses and then those of the rest of the family members: sisters, aunts, grandmothers, and others of lesser importance.

Traditionally, a woman is not expected to protect herself. When a husband and wife are traveling, for example, it is the wife's duty to carry the load and the baby. The husband mostly carries a gun and walks freely ahead of his wife. He cannot be overloaded, for his responsibility is to protect his wife in case of a sudden encounter with an animal, a snake, or an asocial person. It is BaManianga belief that God created woman to bear children and carry on the family lineage, while man is to guard and lead the family group. A woman consents to her role, showing it in her work, talk, acts, and place within the community. Any interference in this arrangement is unwelcome to men and women alike. Hunting, cutting trees, extracting oil from palm nuts, growing rice and cotton, making wine, building houses, marrying girls, protecting the land and the family are man's functions. Planting manioc, peas, beans, and peanuts, gardening, drawing water out of the river, cooking, and caring for children are women's duties. The woman undertakes most of the subsistence farming.[6] Formerly, a woman who happened to be around men was not supposed to walk past them erect; she understood, without its ever being explicitly stated, that she was to pass kneeling down, to express deference to men's leadership. As might be expected, however, the custom is rapidly fading out as more and more women obtain an education. Only some of the older women in the villages still respect the practice.

Each person assumes specific responsibilities according to his or her age and gender. A man is considered an adult when he is able to build his own house and have a wife. Before this, he is restricted to the world of his subgroup. Likewise, a woman reaches adulthood when she is able to get married, although she has no leadership role for the family as the man does. This difference between men's and women's social roles is jokingly symbolized by the fact that the woman cannot have a beard or mustache, as in this song:

> For what cause for what cause
> For what cause
> Women have no beard . . .
> (Mu nkia diambu mu nkia diambu
> Mu nkia diambu
> E bakento bakondolo nzevo . . .)[7]

Men's leadership must not be construed in Western terms as a position of power over others. Power in Manianga society is not something to fight for, to be won in competition. It is primarily a responsibility, and it does not give any man the freedom to abuse others or use violence against them. A man is not believed to be powerful just because he is a man; women are not considered weak or inferior just because they are women. Leadership is a social role dedicated to service; and while it is restricted to men, it does not mean that all men have the capacity to be leaders. Those given such authority in the community are chosen by the ancestors for good character and qualities that will serve the group. In this respect, many men may be in the same class with women in their lack of power. But, like women, they do not have inferiority complexes or low self-esteem because of it. Power in the sense of competitive striving to top others or to have control over them simply does not exist.

In the Kibunzi region, a sister speaks to her brothers, young and old, as *mfumu eto* (literally, "our chief"). He is addressed and respected as chief even before achieving manhood, because his destiny may be to lead.

It may seem paradoxical to a Westerner that the BaKongo family is matrilineal in descent, since leadership rests with men. But that is because the family's survival is recognized as depending on the woman, the childbearer. Conscious of this important social function, most girls have not cared to go to school. Their prime concern has been to get ready for motherhood. That is the major reason why the illiteracy rate among females is very high compared to that among males. To this day there are families who do not allow their girls to go to school. They believe that a well-educated girl will have a difficult time getting married and being a good mother. Proud of her education, she may never accept her traditional role and place.

There is a good portion of truth in this assessment. Some male university graduates, for example, avoid marrying a woman with equivalent education. Economically, intellectually, and culturally, they would feel uncomfortable with a wife who does not follow the traditional pattern. Others, however, actively look for a woman with an education equal to or even higher than their own. Many women university graduates either marry outside Manianga society rather than accept the traditional role or do not marry at all.

The Cohesiveness of the Community

The lineage, which descends through the woman, consists of the totality of all the segments that spring from a single ancestress. Sometimes internal conflicts between segments arise, the principal cause being fear of *kindoki,* usually translated as "witchcraft." (Kindoki, which deals with both good and harmful powers, will be explored at length later in this study.) When members of a particular segment, or *kanda,* prosper and death does not strike them, the unsuccessful members of other *makanda* (plural of *kanda*) begin speculating as to how and why their brothers succeed at the same time they themselves are suffering. If reconciliation is not sought swiftly and a degree of equality reestablished, the matter may worsen to the point of splitting the whole lineage. When the lineage is disrupted as a result of mistrust and disharmony, one or more segments may move to a new location. Such division is rare today, though it appears to have been more common in the time of the great migration.

This kind of family disagreement may seem to a non-African as interference or jealousy. But actually it is a social mechanism that works toward keeping the larger family group integrated. Social solidarity, interaction, and the desire to maintain a uniform level of well-being all work against disruption of the kanda. Given this emphasis on hanging together, everyone's foremost concern is the success of everybody. Everybody is somebody whether rich or poor. They all give themselves plenty of encouragement and help in order to make their lineage a complete success. The concern for a brother and sister is far more important than amassing wealth for personal use. When I have, we have; when I do not have, we do not have: that is the formula upon which Manianga society is built. Because of this communal togetherness, it is impossible to find in the same community extremely wealthy or extremely poor persons. The "haves" do their best to assure the standard of living of the "have nots," as Wesley Brown observes:

> In some ways, the kinship ties form a social nexus in which a person finds a kind of social security. When teenage Simon Nkanza came from Kiyala to Kinshasa in search of work, he went to live with his older brother, Alphonse Mfuta, who had a room at 244 Buta Street. Next-door neighbors on the same lot were Pauline Nkusu, his second cousin, her husband and two little girls. The living arrangement was bearable for about two years, but when Alphonse moved to his concubine and she gave birth to a baby girl, it got too crowded. In addition, there was tension with Simon home most of the day with the concubine, while Alphonse was at

work as a welder at Congo Tubes. Finally, a solution was negotiated in which Simon was to live with maternal uncle Pierre Disu in
Kimbanseke Commune. Subsequently he received his meals there
and has finally found a place as an apprentice mechanic, which
may provide income later. There are no welfare checks in the
Congo, nor is there unemployment compensation. However,
since his arrival, one matrilineal kinsman or another has assured
food and housing.[8]

This is illustrated also by the way in which displaced persons in
Africa are absorbed by their extended families rather than becoming refugees dependent on public assistance. Cyril Adoula, prime
minister of Zaire, expelled thousands of BaKongo and other
Congolese groups in the mid-1960s because they were citizens of
the neighboring Congo Republic, at a time when hostile relations
existed between the two countries. These people were forced to
leave behind in Kinshasa their homes and businesses and enter
the Congo Republic virtually destitute. Internationally, it was
feared that they would create an enormous problem for the
Congo government. But instead they were quietly and almost
completely absorbed into their clans and extended families, as if
nothing had happened. A similar situation prevailed when Nigeria
expelled thousands of Ghanians, who also returned to their
homeland to be uneventfully absorbed by their extended families.

The well-being of every member in the family is far more
important than anything else, no matter how troublesome it may
be to work out solutions to problems. Life is a life of togetherness.
Julius Nyerere spoke in the spirit of African tradition when he
said, "The creation of wealth is a good thing and something which
we will have to increase. But it will cease to be good the moment
wealth ceases to serve man and begins to be served by man."[9] In
this spirit, BaKongo who go abroad to work are always sending
home money, clothing, and other useful items to members of
their family who are not as fortunate.

The aim of being communal is essentially the homogeneity and
balance of the group, a group that always wants to see its members equal but not identical. Accordingly, a member has no right
to use others' goods at will. Each member is to undertake his or
her share of the hard work. The person who makes no great effort
to improve at least his or her own life, who sits waiting for others

to help, will simply vanish helplessly. Begging, when no personal effort is first attempted, is seen as evil. Only after efforts are unsuccessfully made may a kinsman become a community charge.

Communal Life as the Goal of Existence

The fundamental value of existence is life, life here and life in the realm beyond death. Elements such as love, charity, forgiveness, good fellowship, and concern for one another are viewed as a basis to achieve a good society and are not only esteemed but are greatly encouraged. They are the sole path to the real life. But as in any human society, evil exists in the form of hatred, anger, and resentment. How it is dealt with will be discussed at length further on. Generally speaking, evil is relegated to the realm of witchcraft. Witches and other offenders—the noxious haters of this life—are either reprimanded or forced to become outcasts.

Harmonious social life is the highest achievement at which each person and community aims. For example, because of a crude technology still in use, and to ease the burden of heavy work, people join in small rotary groups—*kimbola*—of about three to five persons. Today we work in my fields, tomorrow or the day after we are in yours: that is the formula of kimbola. It is a very effective method to achieve in a matter of a day or days what a single individual would achieve in weeks or months. Whoever works alone fritters away his or her precious time, but not those in groups. A wise man who wants to build a house invites the whole village to help him. Because of this total mobilization, a house that should take days is built in one day or even less. "Strength lies in union" is a value of Manianga community.

No one speaks of "my life" separated from "our life." Consequently, the community is seen as the raison d'etre of one's being. When the community is, I am; when it is not, I am not. In other words, I am because the community is; without it my existence becomes dull and meaningless. There is no other alternative in Manianga philosophy. The African scholar John Mbiti confirms this essentially African view:

In traditional life, the individual does not and cannot exist alone except corporately. He owes his existence to other people, including those of past generations and his contemporaries. He is simply a part of the whole. The community must therefore make, create or produce the individual; for the individual depends on the corporate group. Physical birth is not enough: the child must go through the rites of incorporation so that it becomes fully integrated into the entire society. . . .[10]

The Clan

The clan—*luvila*—is the nucleus of social organization. The word comes from the Kikongo verb *vila* (to tie, to link, to put together). Luvila is then a community or collectivity of all members, alive as well as dead, descended from a common ancestor.[11] As J. van Wing defines it, "The clan is a collectivity of all the uterine descendents of a common ancestress who bear the name of this collectivity. It includes all the individuals of both sexes whether living beneath the earth or on it . . . the deceased and living who have received the ancestress' blood, directly or indirectly. . . ."[12] Van Wing goes on to assume that the founder of the clan must therefore have been female. Although that would seem logical given the fact of matrilineal descent, it is contradicted by the reality that women in Kongo society are not family leaders; there is no evidence to suggest that they ever possessed the power to found and lead their clans. In other words, a matrilinear system does not imply female leadership.

How, then, did the matrilinear system originate? Perhaps the best resolution of the paradox of female powerlessness and matrilinear descent is that proposed by Batsikama ba Mampuya, himself a MuKongo (the prefix *mu* indicates the singular, as *ba* indicates the plural), who has written extensively about Kongo tradition: that the BaKongo became matrilinear through the accident of historical circumstance. I concur with his suggestion that the actual founders of clans were not women but the leaders of the various migrating groups—namely, the uncles. They were the ones who would have led their members and decided where to settle. Their sisters and nieces settled with them, too, but once married they moved to their husbands' clans, living outside their original clan and village. When their marriages ended, either because of death of the husband or divorce, they returned with their children to their own village, which was their brothers' village. Descent then passed naturally through the mother rather than the absent father.

The situation was further reinforced by the nature of male-female relationships in marriage. When polygamy was common, a man's prime concern was to have several wives and many children. He was not inclined to look after them, however, since he was not attached to any particular family group. Each wife was expected to rear her own children. To the father, the children were more or less aliens. In some regions that is still the case today. Therefore he could not lay claim to them after they were grown. The mother became the only legal owner. Whenever she left or divorced her husband, she went with her children. Alienated from their father, they had no alternative but to identify with their mother and her clan.[13] In a system where the paternal role is not emphasized and where the mother and her brothers bear the chief responsibility for rearing children, it is perhaps inevitable that matrilinear descent should form the basis of the clan.

It also follows that in Kongo society there is no family name to be handed down from generation to generation, as in the patriarchal culture of the West. Parents and children, brothers and sisters, do not bear a common family name. A name is usually given the infant by the father, but it can be given by someone else well respected on either side of the family. Naming is not important to lineage or family identity. The name often has some personal significance to the one giving it; it may relate to an important event or personal experience. Later, if the individual dislikes the name or feels that it brings bad luck, he or she is free to change it. Names do not have the fixed, legalistic character they have in the West. Birth certificates did not exist in earlier times, and even today many villagers do not register the birth dates or names of children or parents.

To return to the nature of the clan, we can say that each clan finds its identity in the various meanings of the word *Kongo:* the name of the village of the founder of the Kongo people, whom we earlier identified with a hunter; the name of the hunter; the name of the residents of Kongo City, founded by the hunter, echoed in the expressions *Besi Kongo* or *Bisi Kongo* ("from Kongo"); and the name of the migrants whose roots are in Kongo City. Because each clan designates the same pattern of meanings to *Kongo,* all springing from the same source, the clan members continue to identify with their roots,[14] even if living far from one another. Migration continually widened each family group, which later became known as luvila, those who are bound by ties. This is the origin of the Kongo clans. All the members of a clan, whether living in Angola, Congo Republic, or Zaire, remain brothers and sisters; they recognize the common responsibilities of clanship when they meet, whether or not they are acquaintances, as Batsikama points out: "Mpembele in spite of his Zombo accent remains your clan-brother."[15]

The unwritten law requires that when members of the same clan meet they are to have good fellowship and dealings. In diplomatic terms, clan membership can be defined as one's passport to a good or poor welcome in an unknown region. For example, when an individual is traveling in an area where he is unfamiliar, his clan becomes the key which locks or unlocks the heart of this unknown. If he happens to stay overnight in a village, in the evening when everyone returns home he is invited to eat and chat with the host clansman at *mbongi,* a family shelter, where men exhausted by work come to relax, chat, discuss family matters, teach clan tradition to the next generation, or simply doze.

To introduce a guest to the whole group, the host's family chief asks him who he is and where he is coming from. It is an opportunity to make known himself, his village, and his clan. And if there happen to be members of his clan in the village, they immediately inform him that he has brothers, sisters, uncles, children, nephews, nieces, fathers, and mothers in the village. Informed of the fortuitous arrival of their brother, all the members immediately visit him. They become acquainted in a matter of minutes; they ask after brothers, sisters, mothers, fathers, uncles living away from them, of whom they may not even have been aware. To seal his fortunate welcome among his own people, a small party takes place without delay. At bedtime they provide

him with the very best place to sleep, and in the morning they
make ready his supplies for the trip, unsure whether he will be
lucky again to meet other brothers who will come to his
assistance.[16]

A person who for any reason is unsettled within his own
clan-section is entitled to eke out a living elsewhere and live in
any clan-section he is pleased with.[17] The host family is to provide
everything: house, land to cultivate, even a wife in case he is
unmarried. His rights and duties are the same as those for the
members, and he cannot be considered alien.

As for people not having the same clan roots, they are not
brothers and sisters. Unless they become akin by marriage or
other treaties, they are not bound to any social obligation; this,
however, does not mean they may act unbrotherly. Although they
are not brothers, they are friends and are to help one another
whenever there is a necessity. This willingness to share is extended to any human being who happens to be in Manianga
society. That is the main reason why Christianity was well received
in this region, for it taught beliefs already well established in the
culture.

The structure of the clan and the terminology describing it have
been difficult for Western observers to grasp. To put it most
simply, *luvila* is the term for the sum of all various known and
unknown clan-sections. There is no single chief or head of a
luvila, nor is anyone really sure exactly how extensive it may be,
how many members it may include. On the other hand, *kanda* is
the proper term for a small section of a clan. It is visible and well
defined in the village, and it does have a designated chief or head.
Yet Western Africanists have often used the terms interchange-
ably. Van Wing even uses the word *tribe,* a term alien to Kongo
thought and language and one that perpetuates the discredited
notion of primitivism. One finds Georges Balandier attempting to
distinguish between *kanda dya dinene* (the big family) and *kanda dya fioti* (the small family), that is, parts of a single clan-section
living within the same village.[18] He writes:

> The great families are always the creation of one man rich, rich in
> wives and land. . . . Less powerful families place themselves under
> his protection, though they preserve their autonomy. . . . The

largest *kanda* of this kind never includes more than ten small
kanda. In the more populous villages, and those in which several
unrelated fragments cohabit, the minor lineages take the form of
mbogi, "households," where the men of an extended family come
together to eat their meals, rest, and argue.[19]

This statement is quite misleading, based as it is on the European
idea of a "great family" headed by a patriarch and gathering
around itself related units. The nuclear family in the Western
sense, however large, does not exist in Lower Zaire. A man's
kanda, or particular, local clan-section, is neither large nor small
on the basis of his wives and children; they are not part of his
kanda. A wife, together with her children, centers her family unity
upon her brothers, not her husband. Wives and children are
therefore excluded from the husband's family and are not entitled
to use the land as they wish. They are not oppressed, but neither
are they treated on an equal basis. Further, with regard to the
"one man rich . . . in land," he does not own the land—it is the
ancestors' property. It is never private property to be owned.[20] No
one has the right to possess or sell it or to glory in its wealth.

The correct interpretation of the terms *kanda dia dinene* (the
big family) and *kanda dia fioti* (the small family), then, is this:
they are used only when it is convenient to distinguish between
fragments of a clan dwelling within the same village. The "big
family" is simply that which has more members, and the "small
family" is that which has fewer. Sometimes these terms are not
used at all, and the clan-fragments are distinguished by connecting the leaders' names to their groups (e.g., *Kanda dia Ki-Ngoyi
kia ya Mayabu,* the clan-section of Chief Mayabu) or the geo-
graphical location within the village (e.g., *Ki-Ngoyi kia banda,* the
Lower KiNgoyi).

In actuality, such fine distinctions, so dear to social analysts, are
rapidly disappearing or becoming blurred as more and more
young people leave the villages for the larger cities. The shrinking
size of kanda in the depopulated villages means that distinctions
are less important, and villagers merge more closely in day-to-day
activities, relationships, and responsibilities regardless of which
membership they may have in a clan-section. Clan structure and
history seem less relevant to those living in modern cities. Yet the

underlying pattern still exists beneath the surface, exerting a strong influence and commanding loyalty.

The Role of the Chief

The chief of a kanda can be defined as the embodiment of an ancestral power. His choice is based upon ten criteria. He must be a representative senior of his group; be intelligent and wise; understand the ancestors' wishes from their invisible realm; have leadership skills; be free from harmful kindoki ("witchcraft") and discrimination based on lineage descent; get along with other members of the community; and be a strong representative and good public speaker in major events such as marriage, death, and land disputes. He must be a hard worker; in a society where welfare checks and unemployment compensation are unknown, the chief is to stand ready to feed any person whether from within or outside the group who otherwise would go hungry, for he is more servant than chief. He must also have children—a man with no children cannot be elected chief. It is an abomination to be led by a childless chief. To be childless in Kongo society is to lack respect. Furthermore, he must know the clan tradition from A to Z; he is the "family library."

As a chief, he enjoys a great degree of esteem when he is free of any suspicion of kindoki. His personality and presence over-shadow the whole group. All initiatives emanating from ancestors are made public by him. He is so respected because he is their revelation and representative. As De Gleene stated,

> the chief of the family in traditional thought is the closest member to the ancestors; because of this, he has religious authority over all the family members. Nobody will oppose his will, for they are all convinced that he speaks and acts in the ancestors' name. Obedi-ence and loyalty toward him are for them natural attitudes.[21]

Appointed by the ancestors, he obeys their will accordingly. They are his power. As long as he is in perfect harmony with them he remains the undisputed chief, entitled to respect and obedience. He is neither a dictator nor a tyrant. He never governs as a military ruler,[22] and his position is not hereditary. His authority is religious and judicial. He is the supreme arbiter in all matters affecting the well-being and solidarity of the whole group. "The chief is essentially a judge," Van Wing writes. "Discussions between members of different clans and even members of the same clan are referred to him."[23] Not only does he arbitrate, he is also the father, as Agnes Donohugh explains:

> The chief is the father of his people, sometimes the mediator between the people and the spiritual beings, the holder of the land by virtue of the stewardship he exercises by permission of the spiritual forces and through him the well-being of the people is assured.[24]

The chief ideally should be the oldest among the elders. But if the oldest man lacks the necessary qualities, a somewhat younger one will be chosen. Being a family leader is not a position of power for which men compete. In fact, if two should be equally qualified, each will stand back in deference to the other, so as not to appear self-interested. The leader is not selected by a vote or appointed by any legal authority; he must be chosen by the ancestors. The wishes of the ancestors are expressed to family members through dreams and other signs. It is an intuitive process of arriving at a group decision based on both psychic perceptions and common knowledge of the possible leaders' characters, the respect in which they are held.

On rare occasions, an outstanding and highly regarded family leader, when seeing that he will not live much longer, will choose his successor and train him for the position. Family members will go along with this without objection, out of their deep respect for his wisdom.

Sometimes, too, the best leader is a man who has gone to the city to work while the family has stayed in the village. If no one else equals his qualities of leadership, he may return to take up the responsibility. Men often desire to go back to their village after retirement from work in the city so that they can give the family the benefit of their wisdom and guidance as respected elders, even if not chosen to lead. And many who cannot return while alive request that their bodies be returned to the village after death so that the linkage with their ancestral place will not be broken. They can return in spirit, even if not in bodily form. Even the body of someone who has died abroad may be returned to the village. No matter how far modern villagers may scatter, they maintain their sense of continuity with both the ancestors and those who come after them.

The group is regarded as wise or unwise according to whether its chief is thought wise or unwise. Whether he proves to be up to his function or not, he cannot be criticized. As the saying goes, "Even if ears can grow up they cannot overtake the head" (Makutu kana makudidi ka malendi vioka ntu ko). That summarizes the whole thought of Manianga people vis-à-vis the leader. He is the living ancestor, the one who links the community with the world of the beyond.

The Flow of Living Power from the Ancestors

The well-being of the community, the fertility of the soil, and individual successes or failures depend on ancestral blessings. An inexplicable misfortune or epidemic is enough to make people speculate that the cause is the breaking of the covenant between human and spiritual beings: either all members have acted contrary to the ancestors' expectations and orders or at least one of them has done so. To be restored to peace, health, and prosperity, the broken covenant must first be restored, the essential condition being the recognition and confession of the wrongdoing. The whole group, including members who have moved away from the village, is expected to make arrangements to attend this "life-death" ceremony. Led by the chief, the people pay a visit to Makulu (the ancestors' rest home, or burial place) with sacrifices, a goat (if affordable) and palm wine, to seek mercy and forgiveness.

This sacrificial rendezvous becomes a joyous encounter between visible and invisible worlds. It is also an occasion for the human world to reaffirm its dependency upon the good will of the other world. Then the chief beseeches the ancestors in words such as these, which I recorded at one of the many restoration ceremonies I have attended:

> Do not be surprised to see us here today. We are encountering many inexplicable sufferings, difficulties and mischances. Our

sisters are neither getting married nor are they bearing children. The land is unproductive. We beg your pardon and blessings. Let our sisters be attractive so that they may get married and bear children. Is this not your wish? If we have violated your will, please forgive and clean us like *mvula zampembe* [literally, "white rain," i.e., hail]. Here is your palm wine and . . .

The chief then pours the wine onto the earth and sacrifices an animal when one is available. He sheds its blood on the ground as a symbolic act of self-curse: "If I do not keep this covenant let my blood be shed as the blood of this innocent animal." A domestic animal is always used, since it is considered an integral part of the community. Wild animals excluded from the community are never sacrificed. The sacrifice should bring prosperity and salvation to every living being in the community.

Subsequently the people sing, dance, and return joyfully to the village. They enjoy themselves because from that moment forward they expect their tomorrows to bring what their yesterdays have failed to achieve. Because of this reconciliation ceremony, many Westerners often err by accusing Africans of worshiping the dead. This is a groundless accusation. They do not pray to the dead but venerate them. This veneration is expressed in the way the ancestors are addressed. The word *sambila* (prayer or to pray) is strictly reserved for Nzambi Mpungu Tulendo (God) and is never used in the ceremony.

Family Relationships

Since the social structure of the community is that of the extended family, an individual in Manianga society finds himself or herself governed by fixed family relationships that are determined by custom. All relationships are defined first by bloodline and then by the distinction between senior and junior status (*ndonga ya bayaya* and *bampangi*).

This is most evident in the relationship between mother and child, the most important of all the kinship categories; for it is through the mother that the blood of the family descends. In contrast to Western culture, where the mother–child relationship is perceived in terms of the two individuals, in Kongo culture "mother" is a broader category that includes not only the biological mother but her sisters and brothers as well. "Mother" is a whole stratum of the family. This is revealed in the terms of address used among children and the maternal family members. The child calls both mother and aunts *mama,* and expects to receive the same kind of mother-treatment from all of them. And the uncles, the brothers of the mother, are called *ngudi nkazi* (literally, "male mother," *nkazi* being a word that signifies maleness). The mothers (i.e., the biological mother and her sisters) all call the child *mwana.* The uncles call the child *mwana nkazi* (literally, "male child of the mother") or *mwana nkento* ("female child of the mother"). The aunts and uncles are expected to respond to the demands of their sisters' children and give to them what they want or need the same as the mother would do. Indeed, the uncles give more freely and unequivocally to their sisters' children than they do to their own. But the uncle's children, of course, are in turn the chief responsibility of his wife and her brothers rather than of himself. I and my brother in North Carolina are frequent recipients of letters from our sister's children, some of whom we do not know, demanding that we send them things we cannot even afford for ourselves.

The bonds uniting the maternal cluster of relatives are thus very tight, and the child is obligated to express equal respect to all these senior members of the mother-group. Regardless of their social functions or their standing in the larger community, the child evenly respects and obeys them. If he or she willfully disregards any one of them, the one neglected may sue the child by law. While they are settling their differences, the rest of the community remains neutral.

We come next to the father and the position he and his brothers and sisters occupy in the family group. Like "mother," "father" is also taken in a collective sense; he and his brothers and sisters are evenly respected and obeyed. But here the similarity ends. The children of the father and his siblings are not considered brothers and sisters but rather cousins. Until recently, an exchange marriage, *vutula menga* (literally, "to return blood"), between a son and his paternal aunt's daughter was possible. It was the concrete thanksgiving he could offer to his father's family for the children his father had given to his mother's family, his mother's family being of course his own. By marrying into his father's family, he subsequently strengthened it by the number of children born to his wife. It was well esteemed by the family concerned. Nevertheless, it was a very courageous step for him to take. He had many inconveniences. He had to respect his wife as a father. He could not divorce her or keep her in the kitchen. He could never profit from her daily earnings without her approval. He became almost a slave in his own house.

In earlier times, the community also approved marriages between those who in the West would be called third cousins. In other words, a young man or woman could marry someone from the grandfather's or grandmother's line of descent, as long as he or she was not in the same bloodline. One of them had to be from the father's side, one from the mother's. Such marriages, similar to those of first cousins described above, were also considered disadvantageous.

Given the greater distance between persons so far removed in relationship, third cousins even in the same bloodline were occasionally married with kin approval. In such cases, the fiancée had to pay a symbolic fine and renounce her clan. It was considered to be a marriage of desperation, mostly for the woman, who otherwise would never get married. Today this kind of marriage has virtually disappeared.

Matrilineal descent, despite its centering responsibility on the mother, does not mean that the father is powerless vis-à-vis his own children. As long as he is alive, he is entitled to scold, punish, assist, advise, bless, or curse them whenever they scoff at his authority. Dependent children—that is, unmarried children—are to live with the father as long as he and the mother remain together, until they are grown enough to take care of themselves. Regardless of age, unmarried persons remain dependent. They are considered dependent because they are unable to care for others.

It is also the father's responsibility to protect his children from Kindoki ("witchcraft"). A father whose children are often stricken by death deserves no credit from society.

Seniority

Even if educated or wealthy, individuals cannot pass by the people who have helped them become whatever they are. In the presence of these people they must always remain subdued. Whether right or not, they are not supposed to argue with their seniors. This importance of seniority exists not only among BaManianga but in other African societies as well. The individual has always to obey his or her seniors for two main reasons: seniors know more than he or she does, and they are on their way to becoming ancestors.

The relationship of the child with grandparents is strikingly different from that with parents. The basic relation is neither duty nor respect but rather jokes, pleasantries, humor. They are not bound to respect one another, though a certain degree of respect is due to a grandparent by reason of seniority. This is the most interesting category of kinship. While the grandfather jokes with his grandson, his own son is not a man to be dealt with by humor and jokes. He duly respects his son; otherwise he will fall in community respect. No joking is allowed between children and parents.

The distinction between junior and senior operates also among brothers and sisters, again indicated by the terms used: *mpangi* (junior brother), *yaya* (older brother), and *busi* (sister). By birthright the older male enjoys the privilege of commanding the younger with nearly the same authority as the father or uncle. As we have seen, children whose mothers are sisters are indistinguishably sisters and brothers rather than "cousins" as in the West; consequently, they have the same rights and duties to one another as if they were all from the same biological mother. Everyone has many mpangi and yaya.

In contrast, children whose fathers are brothers are not considered siblings. They are not bound by any special obligation among themselves. For example, a child calls his parental aunt or uncle's children not yaya, mpangi, or busi but by other terms which can be translated as "cousin." As far as Manianga philosophy is concerned, they are not brothers or sisters because they do not have the same blood. Among the present generation, however, this tradition is beginning to weaken under the influence of Western custom.

Marriage

Because the continuation of a matrilinear society depends upon its women, the traditions surrounding marriage are of key importance. Even where Christianity dominates the community and even in modern cities far from the village, the traditional wedding ceremony continues to take precedence over any other kind of marriage rite.

Throughout most of sub-Saharan Africa, female infants are valued equally with males because they have the responsibility of carrying on the lineage. In the gender division of Kongo society, males and females are assigned well-defined, separate roles delineating their responsibiliites, but each is considered equal in value to the other: men are to lead, women are to perpetuate the family. There is no conflict or preference between them, for the aim is the welfare of the family as a whole, not of one aspect of it at the expense of another. Men's taking the traditional leadership role does not imply contempt for female nature. Both men and women have specific parts to play in traditional rituals; women are not excluded with preference to men or given less important roles, and are not sheltered or protected as if they were by nature less competent.

Female infants are welcomed because the more girls born into a family, the larger it will become. This will not occur, however, unless they marry when they grow up. Marriage is therefore too important to be left up to individuals. The romantic basis of marriage in the Western world, which has developed only since the late eighteenth century—two individuals freely deciding to marry because they have fallen in love—does not exist in traditional Kongo society.

A young woman does not take the initiative in proposing to marry. This is the responsibility of a young man in concert with his uncles. It is assumed that a young man will marry when he is old enough to take on responsibility for the lives of others. A suitable wife must then be found for him.

The hopeful bridegroom does not search for a wife himself or approach on his own initiative someone he may particularly like. He first talks to a maternal uncle, who must be well respected in the kanda for decency and mature judgment. (If no one meeting that standard is available, the young man may approach his father instead.) He announces that he is ready to start his family. The uncle must be convinced that the young man is able to look after himself—to build his own house, to be a steady worker, to be able not only to feed his wife and children but also to contribute to the well-being of the extended family. The young man must make a successful case for himself and obtain the agreement and support of his uncle before proceeding any further.

After this initial requirement has been met, it is the uncle's task to search for a good and decent woman. It may be that the young man already has in mind a particular woman he would like to marry. But often this is not the case, and the uncle must make inquiries to find someone suitable. In either event, when the uncle has settled on a prospective wife he talks to reputable men of her village, seeking their advice. When he has learned enough to be convinced that she would be a desirable wife for his nephew, he returns to his own family to discuss the matter in thorough detail. When the family members are satisfied with the potential union, a visit will be made to the future wife's family with a formal request for marriage. If both families agree to the marriage, a date for the traditional ceremony will be set.

The future bride's family will present to the groom's family a list of gifts they wish to receive in payment. The more prosperous his family, the heavier the bill. The typical bill will include cash, sometimes equivalent to a year's salary, should the wife's family be particularly greedy (though this is not common); several African batiks for the women, usually "super-wax," the most expensive kind imported from Holland; new suits for the men; and hoes, machetes, Aladdin lamps, several cases of beer and soft drinks, jars of palm and banana wine, plenty of peanut butter, blankets, sheets, and animals such as goats, pigs, and chickens. The heaviness of the marriage bill is one reason why some university graduates cannot afford to marry a woman from their own region but must turn elsewhere to arrange a union that will not be so costly. The husband's family does not wish to be labeled as poor.

The more prosperous members of the groom's family, even those living abroad, are expected to help foot the bill. I and my brother in North Carolina are constantly bombarded with urgent letters requesting money for a nephew's or a cousin's marriage, often from relatives we do not know. Living abroad does not lessen one's obligation to the extended family.

It must be stressed that the bride is not being purchased or forced into marriage against her will. Women are free to refuse, and sometimes do. Occasionally one finds women who choose never to marry. It is important that both sides consent to the arrangement. Later, if the couple find that their marriage is not working out, the wife can withdraw and return to her family, canceling the marriage agreement. In such cases the gifts presented by the husband's family to hers must be returned, at least in part, as a gesture. However, if the husband should take the initiative in ending the marriage, the wife's family has no obligation to return the gifts. (Divorce will be discussed in more detail below.)

Marriage arrangements epitomize the basic principle of Kongo society: in order to serve the well-being of the society as a whole, all matters must be patiently and peacefully negotiated. No one should be forced against his or her will. There is no violence in relations between men and women, and marriages tend to be more stable, divorces less common, than in the West.

The wedding usually takes place on a Saturday afternoon. It is a grand, happy event that attracts people from all over the surrounding area. Members of the immediate family come from great distances, even from abroad if they can afford it. Although it may seem strange to those familiar only with Western-style weddings, the bride or groom (or both) may be absent from the actual ceremony, with proxies standing in for them. This happens when they work elsewhere or live abroad and cannot be present when the elaborate event has been scheduled. After all, it is primarily a ritual in which the principal players are the two families rather than the two individuals.

Proxy weddings are becoming more common as young people scatter from the villages to work, attend a university, or seek to better themselves abroad. In one case familiar to me, the groom, who was working in the United States and unable to return to Zaire for his own wedding, arranged for a cousin to stand in for him, a man who was married with three children. In a similar case, the groom's elder brother stood in for him. The proxy must be a person commanding respect, with a reputation for decency.

Marriages arranged from abroad are becoming more common. Young men working or studying overseas usually prefer to marry someone from their own culture who will share their attitudes about family and marital status. The formal requirements for negotiating a marriage in these cases are generally somewhat relaxed. The young man may write to a brother or even a close friend, rather than an uncle, to search for a wife for him. If such friends or close relatives are in a large city such as Kinshasa, uncles in the villages may not be contacted for help at all, though of course they will be kept informed. Negotiations may go on for several years through the mail as candidates are located, reviewed, and thought about and consent is obtained. The young man living abroad is granted more flexibility largely because he is highly respected in the family for seeking betterment overseas.

Such marriages may be the least expensive for the groom's family. His future wife's family will present a smaller bill, knowing that they will receive a larger quantity of goods sent home by the wife from her more affluent circumstances abroad. These arranged marriages are remarkably successful, even when the bride and groom have not seen each other until she comes to join him.

The wedding ceremony is conducted in the same manner whether proxies or the bride and groom themselves are present. It begins with the pouring of palm wine on the ground to welcome the ancestors. This sets the proper upbeat, joyous tone for the proceedings. (Since palm wine is associated with Catholic usage and also with non-Christian or unaffiliated groups, Protestants will sometimes substitute banana wine.)

After the ancestors have been welcomed, each family's spokesman comes forward in turn to present his case. These spokesmen are always chosen from among the elders of the family, men considered wise and worthy of respect. If no such person is available, family members may hire an outsider to preside for them. The husband's representative first gives a brief history of how the arrangements came about. He then goes over the bill that has been presented by the wife's family, item by item. If the bill is acceptable or has been successfully negotiated beforehand, he

will announce that fact. In case certain items could not be negotiated behind the scenes, he makes a public case for his position:
perhaps the item was too expensive or hard to find, so this or that
will be substituted.

The wife's family spokesman then steps to the center and
responds to the first presentation, accepting or not accepting the
terms. When all items on the list have finally been negotiated and
approved by both sides, the husband's spokesman returns with
the bill and hands over the items one by one, always beginning
with the most important, the cash.

After the two families have satisfactorily completed the agreement and delivery of the gifts, the two spokesmen begin to dance
in a slow and dignified manner. This is an invitation for everyone
to come forward and express their appreciation. Some of the
older married women may briefly dance with them, wiping the
spokesmen's foreheads with a handkerchief to express gratitude
for a job well done. Others step up with gifts of cash. The families
also give them something to express their appreciation. After this,
the role of the spokesmen comes to an end. The families then
feast and drink together for hours. The wife's family usually
provides a great deal of food and drink for the assemblage to
compensate the husband's family for its heavy expenditure on the
bill. There is an element of give and take, or exchange, even if the
major cost is to the husband's family. Food has been so plentifully
provided that many of those present will take a supply home with
them. This underscores the generosity of the wife's family.

In recent years there has been a gradual increase in the propor-
tion of expenses borne by the wife's family. In cases where the
wife is working and earning money or has more education, she
may actually take charge of the arrangements and supply some of
the items on the bill herself, including cash, especially if it is
difficult for the husband's family to do so.

In contrast to Western weddings, with their emphasis on legal
documents and procedures, there is in the Kongo community no
pronouncement that the couple are now husband and wife, no
moment of official union, no marriage license or official record. It
is simply the ceremony itself that seals the union. During the
ceremony the bride and groom (or their proxies) sit side by side
on a sofa or chairs flanked by members of the opposite sex from

the other's family, observing the event. They have no participating role in it. Recently an innovation has appeared in Kinshasa in which the bride is kept hidden until the bill has been settled and the festivities are ready to begin. Then she is led forth to meet the groom. But this is merely a variation on the core of the ritual, which is the settlement of the marriage agreement.

After the ceremony the husband takes his wife with him. She is no longer part of her family. In the event her husband has not been there and a proxy has stood in for him, she will go with a married brother of her husband or with another married male relative and stay with him until she can join her husband.

Those who are Christian will usually have a second ceremony in a church a few days after the traditional one. But it is brief and perfunctory, only a formality. Invitations are not issued, and family members are not obligated to attend. In such cases, the bride remains with her own family until after this second ceremony before she joins her husband or his relatives, for the union is considered not yet complete. Where the wife goes abroad to join her husband, she will also, if Christian, not live with him until a church ceremony has been performed. In the meantime she will stay with married friends or church members.

There is no honeymoon. The day after the wedding the husband and wife will go about their work as usual. She will begin to get acquainted with her husband's family. In the village, the women of his family will take her to the fields she will work in and introduce her to the other young women with whom she will be teamed. While men usually work in their fields alone, women always work in groups based on age. From now on the new wife will be completely one of them. Some families, in fact, will not even let her go to visit her own family except for some critical cause such as an illness or death, even when the families live in the same village on close and friendly terms.

Before Christianity made inroads, polygamy was widely practiced in Africa. Under the influence of the missionaries and churches it seems no longer to exist in the Christian community. But in a sense it has only gone underground, and if one looks one can occasionally find it. What happens is that a few men here and there set up what is popularly called a *deuxième bureau* (second office), meaning a second wife. Westerners see this as adultery, or keeping a mistress. But it is actually only polygamy with a new name. The second wife—though not bound by any ceremony—often lives nearby, constituting a second family with children. They are openly known, even to the first wife, and are neither concealed in shame nor morally disapproved, coexisting in a natural and friendly fashion.

This is yet another indication that while social mores seem to be changing to conform with Western ideas, in reality traditional attitudes and practices tenaciously and quietly persist. Similarly, the white Christian pastor does not know that at night his African assistant pastor may secretly go to consult a *nganga,* or traditional priest. One has to belong to the culture to appreciate how profoundly things stay the same.

Divorce, like traditional marriage, is not a legal matter as in the West. As no documents were signed in marriage, so none are required for divorce. Usually if there are irreconcilable problems in a marriage the wife, rather than the husband, will simply leave, since she has come to live in his house and has no claim on it. He would be expected to remain there. Although formerly she would take her children with her, nowadays some or all of them may stay with their father. Even though they are separated, the husband has an obligation to take care of her and may continue to supply her needs for money, clothing, or food. In one case familiar to me, the wife left her husband in a regional town to go to Kinshasa to pursue her interest in commercial business. They had been together for thirty years. Their divorce consisted of agreeing not to be married any longer. Divorced couples generally remain on good terms. There is no enmity or fighting over child custody or property. Sometimes the former wife may even continue cooking for her ex-husband.

Unlike marriage, divorce does not require any ritual or family involvement. A brother of the wife may step in to inquire what is happening but does not in any real sense participate in the agreement to separate. Only when the separation occurs fairly near the outset of marriage is the wife's family expected to return any gifts.

Involvement of the two families in a divorce may occur in rare cases where the marriage has not been satisfactory to communal feeling in the first place. In one example I am familiar with, a man refused to marry the woman chosen by his family and persisted in his determination to marry a woman he loved instead. His family members reluctantly agreed to go along with him because he commanded their respect. But the couple were unable to have children, and the family felt there was a curse on the marriage, rendering it barren, because of the man's headstrong insistence on having his own way. A "curse" in this instance does not refer to an act performed by someone but to the blockage of blessings caused by going against communal and ancestral wishes. Not only had the marriage failed to bring children, but normal communal sharing and good will, friendly visits among family members, had been adversely affected. The whole group suffered, and the failure to produce children was seen as clear evidence of a wrongful action. Finally the man's family pressured him to divorce in order to restore communal blessings. The two families came together, each with a spokesman, in a kind of marriage ceremony in reverse, which I attended. There was a token recompense from the wife's family to symbolize return of the gifts. A ceremony was necessary in this case because an error that had been ceremonially sealed in the name of the ancestors, to the detriment of the common good, had to be reversed. Ordinarily divorce is not viewed in such a light. Later, both remarried, and both had children. This was seen as a sign that the curse had been lifted, that communal harmony and happiness and the flow of blessings from the ancestors had been restored.

Had a "curse," in fact, been operating? Westerners would doubtless consider this merely a coincidence, a case of primitive superstition, and would regard the couple as tragic lovers unjustly frustrated by their families. But this is to ignore the real force of communal will, which operates in all societies invisibly and unconsciously to shape the lives, the health, and even the deaths of individuals. Larry Dossey, in *Meaning and Medicine,* understands the communal basis of a curse with exceptional clarity, whether the context is the land of Kongo in 1692 or America in the twentieth century. He cites a story told by an explorer of a Kongo native who unwittingly ate a cooked fowl offered to him by the explorer, who assured him (though he was lying and knew otherwise) that it was not a certain wild hen that was forbidden to be eaten by anyone in his society or a curse on his life would automatically ensue. Two years later, when the man learned that the fowl had indeed been the wild hen forbidden by his religion, he panicked and died within twenty-four hours. The curse had separated him from the source of his life: his communal existence.

"Modern societies are not finished with death curses," Dossey writes.

> An example is the way we deal with the elderly, who are effective-ly cursed by the act of growing old and feeble in a society that fanatically values youthfulness and vigor. We behave differently toward the elderly and they know it. Like the person under a voodoo curse, they often cooperate by behaving like an "old person." . . . This "spell" is intensified on entering the nursing home and being surrounded by others under the same curse, who have come to the same place to live out their role as old persons in accordance with the expectations of their own families. Social support and visitation is all too often gradually withdrawn by families: the old person, like the voodoo victim, ceases to exist. . . . Frequently, the only recourse in such a situation is death, in which the old person obligingly cooperates with his curse.[25]

The Kongo community is well aware of itself as a psychic entity, linked with even greater unseen powers, that is capable of bless-ing or cursing the lives of its members, according to their atti-tudes and behaviors. Marriage is so important because it is at the very center of the flow of blessings into both the family and the larger community, the creating of a new life and carrying on the lineage. But while new birth and youth are always desired, it would be unthinkable to pursue them at the cost of those who are old. A balance must be maintained so that no segment of the community prospers in defiance of another.

The Individual

In contrast to Western attitudes, the individual in Manianga philos-ophy is viewed as both a community creation and a communi-ty responsibility. One's existence begins on the day of birth; an unborn self is merely a parent's property. But before being accepted by the community, the person coming into being must first be initiated and oriented into his or her new world, a world in which he or she is to experience countless ups and downs.

For about a month following birth, the child remains confined in his or her own world, the parents' house. Then the nganga, or priest, ceremonially hands the child a pass into society. The child's coming out is a big day for the whole community. Each member participates in whatever way is affordable: presents (mostly food) or nothing more than the fact of taking part in the initiation. While nganga heads the ceremony, the delighted crowd begins to sing:

> Seer show me the way
> Seer show me the way
> Seer help me see.[26]

The priest then introduces the baby to every corner and road leading from and into the village. This introduction over, the participants all leave at the village headquarters whatever gifts of food they might have been carrying throughout the ceremony, to be eaten by domestic animals. The participation by the animals is a symbol that they too are an integral part of the community.

As the child grows up, the group shapes his or her destiny. For example, to make a baby strong, powerful, wise, and intelligent, the mother is to use various kinds of bones in bathing the baby: monkey bones, to be a good jumper and climber; lion bones, to be strong and have patience to catch animals; gazelle bones, to be an untiring worker.[27] The group dislikes using the bones of certain other animals, such as the chimpanzee, for one reason: a child as strong as a chimpanzee might one day become harmful to society.

A child is usually raised according to family expectation and will. Subsequently his or her success or failure is everybody's success or failure. This influence ends only when the individual's life ends. The community has no part in life beyond the gates of death. At death the person gains increasing power over the community as it loses power over him or her.

Tension between the Public and the Personal

As far as BaManianga are concerned, there are two selves: collective and private. Any breakdown between the two produces a personal and social crisis. When an individual is affected by a malaise, the whole group is substantially affected; thus, personal in nature, it is communal in practice. It is felt, experienced, and shared by everyone.

An individual, in both the private and the collective sense, has no final say about his or her own life. Any goal an individual sets up, any activity he or she undertakes, is done in the context of the whole group. The individual is to be aware of what the group expects from him or her; he or she acts according to that expectation, that will, those needs. Although the society acknowledges each person as a unique individual with unique qualities, talents, and personality, that does not make him or her independent from others. His or her uniqueness, personality, and ambitions are meaningful only when seen in the framework of the whole. As Benjamin C. Ray writes,

> African views of man strike a balance between his collective identity as a member of society and his personal identity as a unique individual. In general, African philosophy tends to define persons in terms of the social groups to which they belong. A person is thought of first of all as a constituent of a particular community, for it is the community which defines who he is and what he can become.[28]

This is true also of BaManianga. Ray continues, speaking of Western ideas of individual freedom:

> The traditional African view is too systematic for such a doctrine, too logically and dynamically integrated. Freedom and individuality are always balanced by destiny and community, and these in turn are balanced by natural and supernatural powers. Each person is a nexus of interesting elements of the self and of the world which shape and are shaped by his behavior. Different societies . . . conceive of these elements in different ways, but the moral ideal is generally the same—the harmonious integration of the self with the world.[29]

Inevitably, such submergence of the individual in the community has its negative side as well. This is being felt to a greater
extent as education becomes more common and young people
grow more aware of outside ways.

A male high school or university student often chooses his field
not in terms of his intellectual ability or vocation but rather in
terms of money, so that he can help his kanda (family). His
foremost concern is to know how much money he will get from
his studies to support his people. Vocations in pastorate and
priesthood, for example, are little sought after in Manianga, as
these jobs do not pay enough money for even a single individual
to survive.

I was myself a victim of these circumstances. I was the first
member of my community to attend both high school and university. My prime goal was to study religion, but that caused an inner
conflict on two levels: by setting up a personal goal I somehow
became antisocial, and by being the first educated, my load was
heavier than that of other members and religion was not the
answer as far as financing the community was concerned. Consequently, I had to lower my personal ambitions. I decided to go
to the school of pharmacy—pharmacy being one of the highest
paying professions in Zaire. Each member of my kanda was
expecting a lot from me. In the meantime, my heart was still in
religion and after two years in pharmacy I felt I had no alternative
but to drop out and respond to my personal aspiration. My action
was treated as an abomination and outrage by the whole kanda.
Everybody was distressed, taken by surprise, speechless. My
maternal uncle—a teacher in a Protestant school—was so embarrassed and disturbed that he fasted for three days. A fast in
Manianga society is used only in case of death. I became a living-
dead. Despite this unceremonious death, I stuck to my goal of
studying religion. The only thing which restored my prestige in
the kanda was my coming abroad.

Given the community involvement, personal long-range goals
are difficult to realize in terms of the traditional life. Day-to-day
living is the common concern. Being communal, an individual in
traditional society alway exists not in terms of "I," the subjective
part, but rather in terms of "we," the collective part. The collective
part far overshadows the subjective one. Therein the male in-

dividual knows not who he is, what he would like to be and to have, where he would like to settle, whether he would like to get married and have children. He implicitly follows the community decision-making process. Everything he does is either proposed or dictated or both. When he comes of age, his maternal uncle betroths him to a girl; whether he likes or dislikes her, his expected response is a firm yes. He dies in his multitude of functions and roles. Fortunately, this daily death does not bother him, for he identifies with his world—the community that has raised him to whatever status he has achieved. Regardless of who he is or what he has, he remains four-fifths communal and one-fifth personal. Such extreme domination of the individual has, as we have seen, yielded to some extent in allowing more freedom of choice for both men and women. But it still remains potent.

On the other hand, the advantage of this togetherness is that it rescues the "have-nots" from worry, anxiety, helplessness, hopelessness, and lack of confidence. A man is never alienated from himself, for alienation occurs chiefly in a society where individualism is the formula.

Anything done secretly or publicly is closely related to the whole group. For example, a person stealing or committing adultery acts alone, but the burden of his or her act is shared by all. In happiness as well as unhappiness, the community good spirit prevails. Nevertheless, the support of a wrongdoer does not mean approval of his or her actions. As he or she has ruined everybody's pride, justice is then to be uncomplaisantly carried out. The BaManianga view is comparable to that described by Junod: "The Bantu possess a strong sense of justice. They believe in social order and in the observance of the laws and, though these laws are not written, they are universal and perfectly well known. The law is the custom, that which has always been done."[30] What is best for the whole group is best for everyone.

In contrast to the West, where a person's property—house, car, clothes, money, children, and so forth—is a part of the private self as much as is his or her own body, in Africa a person's property is part of the community. The African in general and Manianga in particular lives not in the shadow of what he or she has but in the light of what he or she is, the formula of his or her being.

II

THE COMMUNAL RESPONSE TO DEATH AND MISFORTUNE

Death by Natural Causes

Death is the great disrupter of communal harmony. The Manianga community deals with it in two general ways, depending on whether it is natural, that is, the result of old age or other inevitable factors, or whether it is an untimely interruption that can be attributed to kindoki, the exercise of invisible powers.

Death due to age is gladly accepted as natural, for it is initiated by Nzambi Mpungu Tulendo—God. BaManianga hold God responsible for initiating and introducing death. He not only creates; he takes away what he creates. As they say, "God, it was good to fashion us but it was wrong to give us death" (Nzambi bubote wasa mukutuvanga ka mwanki bubi buwatutudila lufwa).[1] To understand this, we must turn to the people's mythical exegesis of death.

BaManianga believe that the first man God created was called Mahungu, from the verb *hunga,* "to carry away." He was a bisexual being, able to procreate by himself. He was *muntu walunga*—a complete being to whom God entrusted the management of the whole creation. He was more powerful than the ancestors, for God's will was to make him *alter sui*—"another himself."[2] Unfortunately, Mahungu would never keep his place. He was so talkative that he began to reveal God's secrets to other creatures, chiefly the animals, saying, "Here is what God intends to do tomorrow" (Lutala Nzambi makana vanga mbazi). And since it was not God's plan to reveal his secrets to creatures other than Mahungu himself, he began to make new plans. Man at that time

36

lived with God; God provided him with everything he needed to survive. He did not have to work; every day he slept or sat around the fire thinking that God must have nothing else to do than to take care of him. Constantly annoyed, God became angry and decided to terminate his friendship with man, since man was unable to hold in confidence what God told him.

So God withdrew and no longer intervened directly in human affairs. As might be expected, his departure was too much for Mahungu, who became helpless. To save him from misery, God introduced a new element to the creation, namely, death. BaManianga, then, interpret death due to natural causes as salvation, because through it man again becomes God's partner. When a man worn out with old age dies, God is the cause; therefore, nobody weeps. God has called him, for his days in this very painful world have been completed. This death is usually peaceful.

Nevertheless, one encounters a difficulty in determining at what time a person becomes aged. Owing to heavy manual labor, some younger adults in their thirties and forties look twenty or thirty years older; on the other hand, there are elders in their seventies or eighties who still flourish with the freshness of youth. In contrast to the Westerners' efficient system of recording age, Africans generally record neither birthday nor birthplace. Most villagers know their approximate age. But it is improper to ask someone, "How old are you?" for he does not know what you are talking about. As a result, everyone's "happy birthday" is celebrated communally on the first of January, as if everyone were born on this date. Even those who were born in a hospital sometimes encounter the same lack of an official individual birthday when the hospital fails to give them a birth certificate. Because of this impreciseness in determining age, an individual is accepted as old enough for death only when he is completely worn out and has no strength left. A strong old man's death is never attributed to God.

Among other Kongo groups, a somewhat different myth explains the origin of death. In this version, God sent the first man into the world bearing a tiny green leaf of *kimbanzia,* a sacred plant that is used to heal and to save life. Then he sent a second man bearing a dead leaf, a symbol of death. The human race chose the dead leaf, or death, because it was afraid of immortality. It was better to exist for a while and then join God than to live forever, not knowing how one would be able to cope with advanced old age.

Yet another version is reported by Thomas Louis Vincent:

> God created man to live forever. No death. He wanted to see if men were wise. He came with two packages that he put before them, asking: "Do you want the package of death or the package of eternal life?" Men chose the package of death because they were afraid to become too old and to support the infirmity of old age. God after observing their choice withdrew, angry.[3]

In all these stories, responsibility for initiating death is divided between human beings and God. God created death, but human beings either chose it or brought it on themselves.

The kimbanzia leaf deserves a further comment, for great significance is attached to it. One hears expressions such as these: to chew kimbanzia is to bless, to forgive, to give life; to be tied or bound with kimbanzia is to be forgiven, saved, blessed, protected; to offer kimbanzia is to calm, to appease, to cause anger to die down; to cut kimbanzia is to confirm, to agree, to soften a blow; and to ask for kimbanzia is to seek a remedy. Kimbanzia is heavily used to cure all sorts of diseases and social malaise. For example, when there is a confrontation between different segments of the community and the chief displays his kimbanzia, all must immediately stop fighting and arguing, for this is a sign that he wants to see peace, not death or bloodshed.

The Response to AIDS

An epidemic of deadly disease such as acquired immune deficiency syndrome evokes a response in African societies very different from that in the United States. It reveals a fundamental attitude of the community toward victims of disease and misfortune. In the United States, a person stricken with AIDS often shocks and frightens others. They are revulsed by the illness and want to expel its victims from society, to get rid of them so they themselves will not be contaminated by their presence. The first question asked is "How did they get it?" Much effort has been spent on trying to trace the origin of the disease and to place responsibility on segments of the population. It is as though public health were a kind of purity that must be maintained by isolating those who pollute it.

In Africa, the response has been exactly the opposite. Instead of "How did they get it?" the question is "How can we help?" It is not a matter of placing blame but of drawing together to cure. I know of a family in Kinshasa, one of whose daughters turned to prostitution and contracted AIDS. No one criticized, accused, or condemned her; no one speculated about how she became infected or felt threatened by her illness. It was not that people were unaware of how AIDS was transmitted; that was secondary to her need for care. It was seen as a misfortune, to be treated compassionately. She received full family and community support and sympathy. For the family does not stick together only in times of happiness: setbacks often serve to strengthen mutual support. The main objective is to save the stricken person if possible. And if that person should die, he or she will die knowing that relatives have done everything they can to help. Illness and death are the concern of all. The sufferer never loses his or her close relationship with the group.

This continual inclusion of the individual in the embrace of the community also means that clinical depression, so common in the United States because of a sense of isolation, is virtually nonexistent in Manianga society. Suicide is unheard of. There are no traditional stories about suicide or even terms for it. Life is sacred, and no one has that kind of control over his own death, which, as we have seen, comes from God. Those who suffer misfortune are not outcast and allowed to become homeless, or abandoned because of old age.

The only true outcasts are those who willfully choose to go outside the traditions, without respect for the communal values that are determined by the ancestors. They are outcasts by their own choice. This must be borne in mind in the following discussion of witchcraft, or kindoki. While support for the victim of misfortune always come first, suspicion can be aroused that some antisocial force is behind the occurrence.

Death Due to Kindoki

Because of limited belief in bacteria, viruses, malnutrition, or uncleanliness as causes of disease, almost any kind of disease or accident can be attributed to unhappy spiritual beings or to human beings endowed with mysterious powers to do harm. If a person is killed by lightning, for example, a factual explanation is never accepted. Concerned kin are suspicious and want to find out why lightning has deliberately struck their relative and not some other individual. In 1958 my distant cousin Nsumbu Aaron was killed by lightning in one of the most ferocious tropical storms in the area that year. Since he was with two elder members of the family, one of them a renowned *ndoki* (practitioner of kindoki), there was no doubt in people's minds that he was killed by that man's kindoki, or invisible power to do harm.

In such cases, inquiries concerning the real cause or causes behind the death are made. The investigative process is to debate questions such as "Why did he go out while it was raining?" "Was he alone?" "Who saw him first?" "Was he killed instantaneously?" Even if a person suspected of being ndoki was in the neighborhood only by chance when the accident took place, he becomes the number one suspect. He is compelled to explain what he knows. If he claims to be innocent he will be made to face *ngang'a ngombo,* the priest-specialist in discovering causes of misfortune. In the pre-Christian era such a suspected ndoki was given a derivative of a poisonous plant to drink. If he prevailed over it, he was immediately acquitted; if it downed him, he was guilty and was to be burned alive the same day with the body of his supposed victim. Because of Christianity, the use of poison was discontinued and ngang'a ngombo took over.

But invisible spirits, rather than living individuals, are most often credited as the causes of illness or death when they seem complex and unidentifiable. However, since it is difficult if not impossible to identify positively which ones are at work, to avoid vexing the suspected spirit, who might not be the cause, the case quickly draws to an inconclusive end. The spirits are responsible, and yet they cannot be impeached. The more complicated the disaster, the more suspected they are.

Present-Day Belief in Kindoki

The belief in other causes of death does not lessen the belief in kindoki. Even among highly educated BaManianga, belief in the possibility of such influences continues to exist. I prefer to use the term *kindoki* rather than the English word *witchcraft* because BaManianga make no distinction between who is a witch and who is a sorcerer. Some are born ndoki, noticed by everyone even in childhood, and others, potentially as harmful, become ndoki only later on.

Evans-Pritchard says that the Azande make a distinction between witchcraft and sorcery:

> A witch performs no rite, utters no spell, and possesses no medicines. An act of witchcraft is a psychic act. They [the Azande] believe also that sorcerers may do them ill by performing magic rites with bad medicines. Azande distinguish clearly between witches and sorcerers.[4]

BaManianga make no such distinction between those who use psychic power and those who use medicines and spells. They have only one term, *kindoki*. To translate this as "witchcraft," "sorcery," or both would obscure the true meaning of kindoki, given the acceptance by many people of the differentiation of the terms. Kindoki is simply the art of exercising unusual powers.

Belief in kindoki provides for the expression of fear, peace, security, anxiety, insecurity, failure and success. No one can claim to understand Manianga society while being ignorant of this phenomenon. To ascertain whether the belief in kindoki is stronger or weaker today, I interviewed many BaManianga and wrote to many others whom I could not reach personally. The question I asked was "Do you believe in kindoki?" All respondents living in villages replied that they did; among those living in cities, a few disbelieved.

From these interviews, letters, and interpretation of my field notes, it is appropriate to conclude that among BaManianga living in villages, whether Christian or not, everybody believes in kindoki; in cities and abroad, while most of the old men said that they believed in kindoki, most of the young men said that they did not.

Eighty percent of the old men in the cities were either born in villages or go there from time to time. On the other hand, most of the young men (though by no means all) who are born in cities often are ignorant about kindoki. They become acquainted with its existence during important events, such as death and periods of mourning and illness, or when they are on vacation visiting their relatives in the village. When city dwellers come to visit, *bandoki* (plural of *ndoki*) do not waste any time welcoming them. For example, in 1955 my half-brother Philemon's three children living in Kinshasa accompanied their mother on vacation to the village. The eldest child, who was about ten years old, could not sleep. Whenever it was time for bed he began to cry, for he was so frightened by bandoki who were trying to catch him. He grew thin and was rushed back to his father in Kinshasa. Since then he has never dared to return to the village. The second child, who was about five years old, became deaf and dumb. His deafness and dumbness are attributed to kindoki. His parents claim that before going to the village he was talking; after returning to Kinshasa he could neither talk nor hear. Their father, a charismatic Kongo prophet who has devoted his life to living according to God's expectations, has ever since then denounced kindoki for his children's sufferings.

I also compared Christians with non-Christians. All non-Christians unhesitatingly affirmed their belief in kindoki; a good portion of the Christians (mostly those serving the church) were perplexed by the nature of the question and simply said that they did not believe in kindoki. In this group, the impression which struck me most strongly was the cowardice among certain Christian leaders who publicly reject kindoki as nonsense but privately acknowledge its effects. With the exception of Pastor Bahelele, a retired minister of the Evangelical Church of Manianga, who sees no conflict between being Christian and believing in our traditional heritage, all pastors with whom I talked gave me the impression of not saying what they really thought. For example, I know a childless pastor (whom I shall not name here, out of respect), who after many years of expectation that God would honor his prayers, began to seek help from a nganga, or traditional healer. He then took a second wife and successfully fathered several children. He became inactive in the church because of his resort to polygamy to solve his problem. If all BaManianga could be honest with themselves, it would not be misleading to say that regardless of their religious beliefs or social status, all believe in kindoki. They may behave in a fearful fashion and deny their belief because Westerners have taught them that to believe in their African tradition is to say no to social evolution and progress; that is, to remain *musenzi,* a worthless individual. In the eyes of Westerners, to be regarded as musenzi is worse than being regarded as a monkey. Consequently, an *évolué* who is proud of being the "European" or "North American" of Africa is not ready to compromise his or her status by openly supporting traditional beliefs.

Kindoki: The Unique Power to Do Good or Evil

Buakasa, who studied the BaNdibu, another Kongo group, defines *kindoki* thusly:

> *Kindoki* signifies power or force. The usual meaning denotes this power as evil. But it is susceptible to being exercised in any sense, in a good sense as well as evil. It is a question of an ambivalent, ambiguous power, which arouses fear; of a dangerous and good power, capable of harming but also protecting.[5]

Generally, any member of the community with unique qualities may be considered ndoki, possessing this power. Whoever succeeds in his or her daily routine becomes ndoki. In this way, a successful farmer is ndoki, a responsible leader is ndoki, a good wine-maker is ndoki, a lovable individual is ndoki, a good trader is ndoki, a good driver is ndoki, a good politician is ndoki, a famous judge is ndoki. Hence, kindoki can be termed a quality which makes a particular human being different from the average or ordinary person. This quality overshadows his or her many failures, and he or she becomes the community's symbol, for any outstanding success must be due to the exercise of some kind of unique power. "Good" kindoki, unlike its harmful counterpart, has no need of secret organizations or rites, for it flourishes in the daylight world of normal society. It expresses the best and most admired aspects of the community.

It is traditionally believed that a man whose special quality is not in the field in which he is engaged, but lies elsewhere, will only encounter failure. The following case is an illustration.

Maboto[6] was a dull student. He could learn nothing and could not pass the first grade. Each year his status remained the same: First-grader. After so many years of failure, he finally became the "dean" of the school, as far as age was concerned. Being the oldest pupil, he was not only continually out of step; he became the butt of jokes and mockery. Even his teacher scoffed at his dull intellect.

To puzzle him, the teacher asked him easy questions everyone was supposed to know. Each day his dullness was the talk of the school. But as everything has an end, he finally took thought of himself and felt deeply embarrassed. He cried, "Enough! Enough! This is D [decision] day in my life, my family and future. I am leaving school right now." Everybody at school, claiming to be stunned, was nevertheless relieved to get rid of his burdensome presence. In his own village, no one cared; he was an accomplished failure. He was the symbol of disgrace to his kin.

Surprisingly, he took heart and refused to give up. Day and night he pondered how he could prove his ability to society. One day at random he accompanied other youths to the market. Roaming around, he by chance met a Portuguese merchant who was desperately looking for a "boy" (helper, servant) to work for him. A good "boy" was expected to be illiterate so he would not be able to cheat his boss. Maboto, however, was semi-literate. His prime duties included cooking, washing and ironing clothes, mopping the house, and gardening. He thanked his ancestors not only for not letting him completely down but also for helping him be associated with a European. In those days people had a high regard for any person associated with whites, who at that time were Africans' exemplars.

Consequently, being associated with a Portuguese, yesterday's wretched Maboto suddenly rose to the rank of a man of note. His lack of success at school did not obstruct his progress as a "boy" at all. He put his heart completely into his job, for he wanted to prove to the whole society that school was not everything. The Portuguese was so delighted by his devotion, punctuality, hard work, and honesty that in a few months he was promoted to the rank of storeroom assistant. This took place in the turbulent year of 1959. A year later Zaire, then the Belgian Congo, became politically free. Frightened by the violence that accompanied adjustment to independence, most whites elected to leave the country; Maboto's boss was no exception. Immediately an unforeseen event materialized: Maboto took over the business. And in less than no time, yesterday's failure found himself a wealthy person. He had money, stores, cars, and trucks—which, understandably, he could not drive. In the meantime he organized his affairs, hired employees and an outstanding accountant to manage finances. His accidental meeting with the Portuguese merchant brought about a complete turnaround in his life. He became a famous person throughout the area.

As expected, his wealth now attracts everybody; brothers, sisters, nephews, and nieces moved to his house to enjoy it. His father, a former farmer, is now a successful itinerant merchant. With no ill feeling, Maboto gladly assists whoever is in need. In 1970 he built for his former school one of the most beautiful buildings in the area. Out of a despised life, he became successful for one reason: he discovered his quality, his kindoki. This is the kind of kindoki every community wishes its members to have.

Speaking of kindoki therefore does not necessarily refer to evil. It is inaccurate (at least in Manianga understanding) to define it solely as harmful. An evildoer is ndoki, a benefactor is ndoki as well. They are both ndoki in their undertakings and approach to the community. They are ndoki for what they do; that is, their particular specialty cannot be handled by any other member of the society. They are ndoki both by their acts and by their uniqueness, which can only be explained by their having the gift of unusual powers.

Harmful Kindoki

Kindoki comes from the Kikongo verb *loka,* "to bewitch"; as Masamba writes,

> The verb *loka* in Kikongo is the only one used to designate the
> action of bewitching, by an unknown person, some destructive

power upon a person. When a parent pronounces publicly some malediction against a member of the clan, the verb *siba* is used. One who is suffering from *kindoki* or *nsibu* is cured by the same acts of reconciliation. . . .[7]

Masamba seems to be saying that the verb *loka* is used solely to designate hurtful acts by an undetected ndoki. This is not the case in other parts of Manianga, where *loka* is also used to designate the action of a father who curses his son or daughter.

Although the verb *loka* is the root of *kindoki,* it is not always used among BaManianga in talking about harmful kindoki. Instead, the verb *dia,* "to eat," may be used to describe ndoki's actions. It is believed that ndoki mystically eats his victims.

Harmful kindoki, unlike good kindoki, does not operate openly. It is a half-hidden institution within the community into which its adherents are initiated before birth or in early childhood when their reasoning powers are undeveloped. The practitioners of that power, those who are ndoki, form a kind of shadow community, echoing the pattern of the true or "good" community, but in reverse. They are dedicated to doing harm instead of helping and protecting the group. This secret community is not fully known or understood. It is hidden and mysterious, known completely only to ndoki themselves. Occasionally ndoki's secrets are revealed to outsiders under special circumstances, as we shall see; but to know fully how they operate, one would have to be an initiated member, pledged to secrecy.

In the following account of how the community handles harmful kindoki in its midst, it should be kept in mind that evil tendencies are considered an inescapable part of human nature, not something that can be completely eradicated. Such tendencies can only be integrated into the community and kept under control. Christian missionaries have been quite unsuccessful in their attempt to destroy belief in kindoki because the people do not have the idea of purity as a goal, or of warfare against sin, requiring evil to be cast out. All human beings, it is understood, are a mixture of good and bad to varying degrees. No one can attain perfection in this life. That is possible only to ancestors in the after-death world. Since everyone has both a good and a bad side, the goal is to keep the bad side under control, not to let it become worse than need be. The community in order to prosper must be in harmony with its own evil side, just as the individual must strike a successful balance between strengths and weaknesses. Harmful kindoki is allowed a well-defined place in the community so it can be subjected to the checks and balances that keep the group unified and thriving.

BaManianga clearly distinguish between *kindoki kia dia* (literally, "eating kindoki") and *kindoki kia lunda* ("protecting kindoki"). When it is used to do harm, they fear and denounce it. Any ndoki suspected of harming others is disliked or hated at the time he is harming. But when he is at peace, that is, when no one is sick, dying, or experiencing misfortune, the community more or less forgets his wrongdoing and welcomes him into the family like any other member. Like any other nonevil ndoki, he is to be loved and cared for as if he had a clean record.

Besides their differing aims and methods, a major difference between "eating" kindoki and "protecting" kindoki is that while the latter operates openly and in broad daylight, the former is secretly conducted at night behind closed doors while everyone sleeps. It is perceived as *ngangu*—intellect and force. Any individual can possess natural intellect and force through will and personal dedication, without threatening the fate of the community; but these "night intellects and forces" are in disharmony with positive forces because they are the property of the night. They are possessed only by night ndoki. In other words, night kindoki is dark as the night, whereas day kindoki is bright and clear as the day.

The adherents of night kindoki, being the failures or upstarts of the community, are viewed as merciless toward their victims, whom, in actuality, they are afraid of. Since they fear them, they are impelled to send them death or incurable disease. At night, ndoki has no heart, that is, he does not know how to forgive another. The Manianga belief is that this type of kindoki is carried out by both human beings and bad spirits. As to the question of how they operate, BaManianga seem somewhat inconsistent. First, there is the belief that ndoki destroys his victims by eating them; he invisibly attracts their psyche, their inner source of life and vitality. And yet the belief in life after death is never doubted. Then how can we relate these two contradictory beliefs? Masamba replies:

The verb *loka* is not popularly used in talking about the activities of *ndoki*. The verb *dia*, to eat, is used when, in a mystical way, a *ndoki* has bewitched a human being. These expressions are common: *Wamana diwanga kala* (he has already been eaten); *Bila nki badilanga bantu kimoyo?* (Why do they eat people but still keep them alive?) *Ndoki kadianga wangani ko* (*Ndoki* never eats a stranger). *Dia* means to kill, to attack metaphysically; it does not always represent an anthropophagia mania as some anthropologists have tended to think.

Here are two reasons that seem to be at the root of the use of the verb *dia*. First, *vonda* (to kill) and *loka* (to give poison) are physical acts, which could be performed only by using violence. They represent expressions of hatred, representing a slow process of being killed by one who is your own, yet hates you. As *dia* enters into the realm of psycho-metaphysical "eating-up," the patient can react to it by a process of counter-reactions.

Secondly, to exchange food among members of the same clan was the order of traditional clanic living.[8]

What Masamba claims here is that at night ndoki is one who eats metaphysically, without, however, explaining what is eaten or even how it is eaten.

To me the question is very deep because when people in the village talk about kindoki kia dia they do not think metaphysically. I have interviewed many villagers to ascertain if it is possible for a ndoki to eat his victims in a society where anthropophagy has never been practiced or detected. Surprisingly and unexpectedly, one respondent told me: "Out of ignorance you do not know that night ndoki and non-night ndoki do not belong to the same world. They live in two unassociated worlds. What the society forbids is not ipso facto forbidden in the world of the night ndoki."[9] He then invited me to attend a ritual ceremony at which an alleged responsible ndoki was to be denounced. The case took place while I was touring through Manianga to do research on my thesis in the summer of 1972.

As usual, when a family is impaired by disease, death, or inexplicable misfortune, the shortest road to peace is to consult nganga, or priest. In this particular case an important member was very sick. To save him the concerned family members were urgently convened. After unsuccessfully attempting to ferret out the cause or causes, they called in a charismatic diviner named Dieudonné (literally, "given by God"). He considers himself a prophet sent by God to save Manianga in the way Old Testament prophets were sent to Israel. He is chiefly a diviner. He displays neither wonders nor miracles. His foremost task is to denounce ndoki and to foresee any unfortunate event to come.

Before his arrival, the family leader gathered his people in the house. Everyone else in the village was also compelled to attend, and, as expected, everyone was there. As he was coming into the house, Dieudonné asked to have a pail of water placed in the middle of the room. Everyone in the family was to stand in front of that clean water and say whatever he knew about the patient. As required by tradition, the leader was first to take the stand. Invoking the family ancestors as witnesses, he addressed the patient: "If it is I who am bewitching you, get well immediately, otherwise let me die instead of you. Let all of you be my witnesses." The manner in which he spoke gave two impressions: that he could be the alleged ndoki but was not aware of it and that the invocation was purely a formality to emphasize his innocence.

Afterward he washed his face in holy water. As he was returning to his seat, Dieudonné checked the water to see whether the image of his face could be detected. Whether or not he could see it, he would not say until everyone had had the opportunity to speak. It is uncommon, however, for a ndoki to reveal his own wrongdoing. After everyone had argued his case and washed his face, Dieudonné went to work. He took away the pail in order to examine the water and catch the evil-doer. Later he emerged with the verdict, the accusation of the ndoki responsible. To nobody's surprise the denounced was Nkombo, a famed ndoki. Whether or not she was the one who was bewitching the patient, there was nothing she could do but agree with Dieudonné's findings. Without delay the patient's closest kin began to push her to do something about the recovery of the patient. Helplessly surprised and confused, she remained openmouthed.

The manner in which the enchanter was discovered left me suspicious with regard to Dieudonné's ability. First, the accused was a renowned ndoki. Throughout the area she was known and feared. Nobody would joke with her; her house was isolated, for to hang around her would mean to risk one's life. Dieudonné knew all these facts. Second, she was a woman out of the common. She had shaky, withered hands which, according to Dieu-donné, he had psychically perceived in the very act of bewitching.

After the handing down of the verdict, I did not regard him as "Dieu-donné," but rather as a farce player. Pointing his fist at her, he threatened her, trying to force her to liberate the victim. To everyone's astonishment, Nkombo confessed her bewitching, claiming that the decision of whom to kill was not hers alone but communal. It was unanimously taken at night at the ndoki's meeting place, *Zandu dia bandoki* (literally, "ndoki's market"), where they meet to conduct their business.

"After selecting the innocent victim, I was chosen to carry out the killing," Nkombo flatly explained. "I have been killing him very slowly, for there was no hurry; otherwise he would have been gone the same day." To Dieudonné's command to free the patient, she would not say a word without first consulting the others. Usually when a ndoki catches a victim, the latter is doomed, and that is what happened to Nkombo's supposed victim. He died within months. Nevertheless, his enchanter did not live much longer either. It was believed that she was killed by her associates for fear of being denounced themselves. To display their dissatisfaction, the victim's kin refused to cooperate any longer with Nkombo's clan-segment.

Conflict among clan-segments may, in fact, result in counterac-cusations of kindoki. For BaManianga, as for the Chewa of Zambia and Malawi whom M. G. Marwick describes,

> tensions between the two segments which may be expressed in
> the form of rivalry between groups, or more specifically between
> their leaders, pass through two phases. So long as the matrilineage
> remains united, segment leaders compete for its overall control;
> and accusations of sorcery have the function of discrediting rivals.
> Once division has started, segment leaders may abandon hope of
> ever achieving overall control; and the accusations of sorcery then
> have the function of accelerating and justifying the incipient sepa-
> ration.[10]

Wesley H. Brown similarly observes of BaKongo: "Witchcraft ac-cusation plays a significant role as sanction, and as a symbol of the extent to which members of a clan-section are linked to one another in times of distress."[11] Any evil ndoki accused of "eating" an indispensable member may be beaten to death if he fails to seek safety in flight from community rage, as in this case from Lower Zaire in 1944, reported by Brown: "In 1944, chief Maya of Kiswemi's natal village, Kiyala, who was accused of 'eating' persons in the village, was beaten and mortally wounded. He finally escaped, staggered some miles away to the railroad station at Bloc 236 and died. . . ."[12] Any individual can be regarded as ndoki in a harmful sense, even if he himself is unconscious of being so, as Evans-Pritchard found when studying the Azande:

> But though many men declare in private that they are not witches and that there must have been a mistake, my experience of Azande when presented with hens' wings has convinced me that some think for a short time at any rate, that perhaps after all they are witches. Tradition about witchcraft is so definite about what cannot normally be tested, e.g., the concrete nature of witchcraft-substance [invisible substance a witch sends out from himself to contact a victim] is vague and indeterminate about what might be proved or disproved, namely, the operation of witchcraft. The manner in which witches carry out their exploits is a mystery to Azande, and since in waking life they have no evidence on which to base a theory of action, they fall back upon the transcendental nature of the soul. . . . It is possible to understand, therefore, that a man accused of bewitching another may hesitate to deny the accusation and even to convince himself for a short while of its evident untruth. He knows that often witches are asleep when the soul of their witchcraft-substance flits on its errand of destruction. Perhaps when he was asleep and unaware something of the kind happened and witchcraft led its independent life. In these circumstances a man might well be a witch and yet not know that he is one. In Azande culture witchcraft is so much a daily consideration, is so much taken for granted, and so universal, that a man might easily suppose that since anyone may be a witch it is possible that he is one himself.[13]

Persons accused of kindoki kia dia are nearly always older, graying members. By "eating" others' life force they are thought to be able to extend their own life force. This, according to folk belief, is the main reason there are more old than young individuals in the villages. While this might at first glance appear to contradict the respect normally given to the old, it will be recalled that the secret community of ndoki is structured like the true community. Therefore, it too has its elders and leaders, those who have advanced to authority through experience and knowledge. Older ndoki are likely to be the most powerful.

An alleged evil ndoki may be forgiven his sin when he confesses it and convincingly explains to concerned members why and how he has been engaged in such activities. They may also require him to pay a modest fine (often an animal) as compensation for the loss or suffering of the victim. They then cut the animal's throat, and the blood is figuratively drunk by the ancestors of the clan-section. This animal blood symbolizes ndoki's own blood. Shedding it, he makes himself available to severe punishment. Whenever he is found guilty, his blood will flow; that is, he makes himself liable to be killed if he should resume his evil activities.

Among harmful ndoki, the deadliest ones are believed to be *minziula* (singular, *munziula*). The word *munziula* comes from the verb *ziula,* "to exhume, unearth." Eager for money, they make it their specialty to exhume recently buried persons to steal and sell their personal belongings: sheets, blankets, and other gifts the dead have received to use in their childhood life in the new world. Generally they go to the tomb at a time when no one is expected to be in the vicinity. Using their evil power, they unearth the recent dead, open the coffin, and take whatever may be of value. Then they go to a nearby river to wash their acquisitions before selling them. At this particular time they are deadly. Any unfortunate person who happens to see them will be mercilessly executed at once, so that he cannot reveal their secret, for otherwise he would endanger their business. To know how they get their goods would mean not buying in their stores. Fortunately, most of them (but by no means all) are secretly known so that no one is willing to enter their stores. For example, at Tadi, a local commercial center near Sundi-Lutete in Kivunda district, there was, at the time I left the area in 1967 to attend the University in Kisangani, a well-known business munziula by the name of Muzenge.[14] Those who bought his goods were mostly his business partners; otherwise he would already have gone bankrupt.

Most ndoki are initiated into the institution of kindoki in early childhood by a relative who happens to be ndoki or even by a mother while the child is still in the womb. But occasionally an attempt is made to claim an older child whose mind has already been formed by community values. Such efforts often do not succeed, and may have disastrous results.

An interesting case occurred in the 1960s in the village of Kimata, about five miles from my own village of Banza-Lele. A husband and wife, both of whom were ndoki, decided to initiate into kindoki their twin children, a daughter and a son. Among BaManianga, twins are always given the same set of names rather than being named in the usual fashion. Whether they are both boys, both girls, or one of each sex, the first child to emerge from the womb is considered the older and is always named Nzuzi. The second, or younger, is always named Nsimba. Anyone encountering a person with one of these names will know that he or she is a twin.

Nzuzi, in this instance, was a girl with a sweet temperament. She was always mild natured, incapable of being angry at anyone. Because she was the elder, she was the first of the twins that the parents tried to induct into kindoki, at about age seventeen. But because of her goodness and sweetness of character, she did not possess enough of the inborn hardheartedness required for her to develop into ndoki. Instead, she was gradually destroyed by the attempt, and died. She was an easy prey to be "eaten," for she was incapable of understanding evil and defending herself.

Then when her brother, Nsimba, was about twenty years of age, his parents began the effort of initiating him into kindoki. Nsimba was different from his sister. He tended to be moody and changeable, with a mean streak in his character. This indicated a "bad" side that might be developed further, to make him a successful ndoki. By the age of twenty, however, most people have developed a balance among the qualities of their character that is not easily changed. Any attempt to lead them into kindoki is likely to result in violent inner conflict as the "good" side resists being overwhelmed by the "bad." This is what happened to Nsimba.

The details of the initiation process are unknown. Probably it involves taking the novice to the ndoki "market," the meeting place where they come to propose people to be "eaten" and to bargain over them without pity. Ndoki can have no heart; they must be willing to sacrifice near and dear ones in their own families. Nsimba responded to his parents' effort by struggling so violently against it that at times he appeared confused and crazy. When in a crazed state, he would tell what his parents were trying to do to him. He did not see how he could possibly become involved in killing people without cause; he was also angry at his parents for what he knew they had done to his sister, and was heard to threaten to kill his father violently by his own hands. During crazed spells he sometimes had to be tied down to prevent him from doing damage or going to look for his father, whom he could not forgive. (He was not angry toward his mother, but felt sorry for her, believing that she only followed the lead of his father.)

After a while he left his father's village and went to live with his mother's family in Banza-Lele. When he was away from his father, he returned to being a normal, pleasant person. He seemed even nicer than before, as if the struggle had actually strengthened his good qualities. But it was difficult to avoid coming into contact with his father on occasion. It was also believed that the father made invisible night visits to try to gain control over him. After any contact with his father, Nsimba would go crazy again and lose control. It was as though he had been taken over by an evil spirit. He would laugh and shout insults about his father, saying, "He tried, he didn't succeed." Afterward he would not remember what had happened.

Usually there is one person in the community who is able to calm down someone in that condition. Nsimba, with help, always managed to overcome these attacks. Eventually his mother's family obtained a nganga (priest-healer) to attempt a cure. As far as I know, Nsimba succeeded in shaking off his father's effort, and eventually married and had children of his own.

The end result for someone like Nsimba is not always benign. Some remain in conflict the rest of their lives, and in fact may not live very long. If the ndoki cannot succeed in capturing him, but will not let go, the victim will remain in trouble. But sometimes the ndoki will decide it is not worth it to continue the struggle and will give it up, as Nsimba's father may have done. In other cases, the ndoki may die, thus releasing the victim. But anyone who is not released by one means or another can never be permanently well. On the whole, attempts to claim initiates into kindoki later in life rather than in early childhood seldom seem to succeed completely. There is too much resistance on the part of the victim. Such incidents still occur, and show interesting signs of adapting to modern conditions.

I am familiar with another case from the late 1980s, in the village of Kingila, not far from Sundi-Lutete. A woman of around sixty had to return to Kingila, her family's village, after the death of her husband, a schoolteacher. During all the years of their marriage he had refused to let his wife or children visit Kingila because it had a reputation for being rife with harmful kindoki. The woman's aunt was well known as a powerful ndoki who had tried to give those powers to her daughter and son when they were in their teens. Both had gone insane. The aunt had worked for years trying to destroy the family of the widow returning to her village.

The widow brought with her a mature daughter, whom we will call Bernadette, in order to protect her identity. The aunt soon determined to capture Bernadette and turn her into a ndoki like herself. Bernadette was not able to put up a strong resistance, though she became confused, mentally troubled, and would do crazy things like running out of the house unclothed. Later she said the ndoki had taught her to fly an airplane, in which she was sent out with a video camera at night to spy on her brothers and sisters and report back on what they were doing.

After a few years Bernadette and her mother, the widow, were brought to Kinshasa to live with another daughter in order to escape from the conditions of the village. Away from the malevolent aunt, Bernadette improved somewhat, confessing what the ndoki had done to her but still talking crazily at times. She was angry, and like Nsimba kept repeating, "They tried, but they didn't succeed." Not long afterward, the aunt died, and Bernadette went to stay with her brother in Kisangani where she could be treated by a woman famous for cures of such cases, using herbs and other methods. Women are often outstanding healers. At last report, Bernadette had improved considerably.

Bernadette's case is noteworthy because of the way in which ndoki have adapted the imagery of modern technology to describe their invisible night flights and methods of spying on their victims. Far from feeling threatened by the contemporary science of the West, they quickly grasp parallels with their own practices and apply them. Bernadette apparently believed that she had literally been able to fly an airplane and use a television camera.

These cases illustrate another important point. Ndoki are not free to attack anyone they please. They are restricted to members of their own family line. Thus they follow the usual family pattern, only in reverse: while a good leader is devoted to being a servant of his family's needs, a ndoki leader is just the opposite. He cannot feel sympathy for anyone; he must be heartless and willing to sacrifice his closest family members.

Sometimes the "day" and "night" leaders in a family end up being the same person. This happens when a harmful ndoki is the only man available to assume the position of family leader, because of his age, experience, and knowledge of family history. This creates a period of crisis for both the family and the leader, who is faced with a contradictory role.

That occurred in my own family. The leader, who had once tried to poison me as a child and had worked hard to do harm to family members, decided upon becoming the leader that he would renounce kindoki and try to become a good person before he died. He was near the end of his life. Some ndoki are not as virulently hateful as others and even retain a modicum of goodness, as this man did. He had long hated my half-brother Philemon, the charismatic religious leader, because he was always afraid of being exposed by him. When he came to Kinshasa for dental work, he did not stay with any of his own children, who were successful in business, but begged to stay with Philemon, who he believed could help him overcome his bad side and thus die as a good person. He lived there for two months. I saw him, took him places where he needed to go, and felt sorry for him. He returned to the village, confessed, and asked to be forgiven. He wanted to assume the duties of a true leader, of protecting and helping his family. Because of his change of heart, he was welcomed and forgiven.

Whereas in the United States a person having been punished

for a crime has great difficulty in being received back into the society, which remains unforgiving and suspicious, among BaManianga, if a person confesses and asks for forgiveness he will be fully restored to the community. The separating of anyone from the community is only a means of getting him or her to return and have a change of heart.

There are even some ndoki who try to do as little harm as possible. They attend the market in order to protect their own family members through negotiation, rather than to sacrifice them. They are known as protective ndoki, and are considered to be of value to a family.

The Cleansing of Kindoki

Inevitably, a counterreacton, an anti-"eating" kindoki movement, arose in the Manianga area. It was called Munkukusa, from the verb *kukusa,* "to confess, to purify oneself, to throw away, to cleanse." Its aim was to liberate individuals from the bondage of kindoki kia dia and help them be "born again." With few exceptions, it was well received throughout Manianga, and flourished through the mid-1950s.

According to the men considered upstanding in my area, Munkukusa was accidentally founded in 1951 by an unidentified individual believed to be Christian, somewhere in Manianga. He was doomed to encounter insurmountable difficulties. Married, he successively lost three children, according to Efraim Andersson.[15] As expected, their mysterious and premature deaths were attributed to kindoki.

Tired of raising children fated to die, the bereaved mother decided to leave her husband, who, in her thinking, was "eating" their children, and return to her native kanda. She accused her husband of being the "great eater" of their children for the reason that they did not belong to him, i.e., were not in his bloodline but hers. Without consulting or discussing the matter with him, she spread this word and groundlessly tarnished his reputation as a decent person. This, however, did not make him bitter toward her. The more she hated and accused him, the more he loved and missed her. He often visited her, but neither she nor her family would welcome him. Whenever he showed up in their village, people would scream, "Ndoki, ndoki, ndoki. . . ." Deeply shaken but not discouraged, he prayed unceasingly for his wife, but to no avail.

Finally convinced that he could never persuade her to return, he concluded that the only remaining way to have a heart-to-heart talk would be to publicly confess that he had indeed "eaten" his children; but at the same time, he would declare that both he and his wife "ate" them by common consent. By doing this, he would cause his wife also to be hated, denounced, and expelled, and she would have no alternative but to make things up with her husband. This was a dangerous plan—for he could be stoned to death—but also an ingenious one. He went miles away to make preparations for the event. As a devoted Christian, he devised the use of a cross in an oath to guarantee that if he should ever again "eat" his children or any other person, he would be mercilessly killed. This cross thus became a symbol of death as well as the symbol of salvation. He took animal and human excrement, grave earth, palm wine, and other objects as gifts to his host family. The reason he used animal and human excrement is not clear; perhaps it was a symbolic casting out of his evil nature, an indication that he would henceforth abstain from looking back to the dark and wretched past.

Once ready, he set off. Aware of the nature of his visit, everyone awaited him with curiosity. As he arrived, he presented gifts to the chief of the family and then dug a cross-shaped trench, at the center of which he mixed grave earth and palm wine to make *nteke* mud. Facing the cross, he confessed his (untrue) kindoki: "I am the ndoki who have eaten my children without apparent purpose. If I do it again, ancestors, God, and all of you who are here be my witnesses, I will not deserve to live again. I should be killed instantaneously."[16]

To seal his oath, he smeared himself with mud from the crossed hole, a sign of self-curse. His confession later became the formula of the kukusa rite.[17] After his ceremony, he urged his wife to do the same, because he announced that they had jointly eaten their children. Annoyed and confused, she denied all the allegations. But as there is no physical evidence to distinguish a ndoki from a non-ndoki, her own relatives began to express hatred and to threaten her, and they did not dare listen to what she was saying in self-defense. As far as they were concerned, she was a ndoki and was to be treated as such. The more she denied it, the more she risked her life. To relieve the tension and save her life, she publicly admitted her complicity. Taking the same oath her husband had sworn, she promised to look not behind but ahead. Her husband thereby clearly came out the winner. She returned with him.

From then on, the movement spread from village to village, area to area, until it swept most of Lower Zaire and part of the Congo Republic. For many, Munkukusa was the answer to their daily nightmares. As there would no longer be disease or death because of kindoki, everyone began looking forward to a happier future; and since this could only materialize through the kukusa rite, the movement enjoyed a huge success. As Andersson writes,

> Kundu [witchcraft-substance] and kindoki, which the people had long suffered under, were to be eradicated. If kundu could be destroyed, all disease would come to an end and death itself would be put to flight. By radically and definitively forswearing all kindoki the blacks who were now threatened with total extinction, would be able to increase and survive. Salvation had come with the Munkukusa rites. For this reason all, from infants to old people on the brink of the grave, must enter Munkukusa, in which was seen the only way to salvation from death. . . .
>
> To get rid of kindoki and stop the ravage of diseases was thus the primary aim of the Munkukusa rites. To this were gradually added other motives . . . such as e.g. that the field-produce should for those who had gone through Munkukusa no longer be eaten up by wild animals. In conformity with old tradition, this too, was thought to be due to the havoc played by bandoki. The bandoki sent their animals, i.e bikonko to the neighbors' fields to spoil these. Similarly, the Munkukusa rites brought luck in the hunt. One would "vonda bibulu biabingi, kadi biabio bandoki bibayam-budi" (kill many animals, for the bandoki would now abandon them) . . . through the performance of the Munkukusa rites the lost fertility would be regained.[18]

Consequently, the foremost concern of every family leader was the cleansing of all members. Whenever a leader sought the kukusa rite, he called back home all those deemed to be under his protection. Even those who had moved to big cities were urged to return, for all were to participate; he would not tolerate any excuse. For example, Masamba[19] was outcast from his community for refusing to kukusa. As far as his understanding of it was concerned, Munkukusa was nothing but a heathen movement. His reasoning was influenced by missionary attitudes toward this important rite. But from what I have heard, the movement cannot be regarded as anti-Christian or pagan, for it is clearly an attempt to Christianize traditional beliefs and practices. For example, before the start of the ceremony a Christian song was sung, such as this very popular one:

> Let us go see the cross
> Where Jesus died for us.
> Where is the Savior?
> He died for us.
>
> Cross, cross
> Where Jesus died for us
> Where we shall leave
> All our wrongdoings.
>
> Where he was tormented
> Dying for us
> We can see love
> From God.
>
> On the cross the Savior
> Broke
> Completely Satan's head.
> He took away his force.
>
> At the tomb Satan
> Is saddened
> To see the Savior
> With his angels.[20]

(For the Kikongo text of this song, see the appendix.)

This clearly shows that the aim of Munkukusa was not to slander Christianity, as some missionaries claimed. At first, initiates of Munkukusa were neither anti-Christian nor antiwhite, but, due to the disparagement of the true meaning of the rite, they broke with Christianity and with whites. All those who refused to take part in the rite were treated as if they were ndoki, and were regarded as tools of the whites. They were so isolated that their life became almost unbearable. To this day, some of those Christians who refused to kukusa are still suspected of being ndoki, of "eating" others.

How the Cleansing Rite Was Conducted

When inhabitants of a village sought to cleanse kindoki, they proposed a date to kukusa to the Munkukusa organizers; then they informed their relatives who had moved to towns to come back to the village. They were required to kukusa, too.

Here is how it was done around 1953 in Banza-Lele, where I was born. On the eve of Munkukusa, almost all adult children of the father's side *(bana bambuta),* led by the family chieftain, went at night to Makulu, the ancestors' resting home, or burial place. This visit had two purposes: to inform the ancestors and invite them to take part in the forthcoming event (since the veneration of family members who now dwell beyond the realm of death is necessary for our well-being, they cannot be caught unaware), and to get grave-earth.

They walked in two lines. They were not allowed to look back because to do so would mean being weak or afraid. They could be stripped of their *mwana mbuta* status (literally, "eldest child," but more broadly *mwana mbuta* includes all those born on the father's side with the potential for leadership). Arriving at Makulu, they encircled the grave of the oldest and most powerful ancestor considered to be the leader of both visible and invisible families. In my clan-section, it was the grave of ancestor Nsuni.

Speaking in the name of all bana bambuta, the mwana mbuta who had at that time achieved some degree of fame for his traditional wisdom greeted them by pouring down palm wine. Then he explained the reason for their visit:

> Forgive us coming
> To visit you at this time.
> The fathers you left us are not well.
> They are suffering,

Old people are dying.
We the children are deeply saddened
To witness their miserable life.
If they are continually dying
In whom will we take pride again?
To end this suffering
As children this is what we have decided:
Tomorrow all our fathers
Who moved to towns
As well as who stayed in the village
Are to kukusa.
Come and be our witnesses.
Whoever is responsible
His verdict is death.[21]

(For the Kikongo text, see the appendix.)

When the speech was over, the chieftain poured wine alongside the grave. Smearing the soil with wine, he created the mud with which he anointed all bana bambuta who made the trip. It was their blessing from their forefathers. They were required not to wash that mud away before the entire rite was ended. In the meantime, the remaining mud was put in a pot and carried back to the village.

As they started out on their return to the village, they fired a gun, a symbolic invitation for the dead to follow behind them; then they began to sing:

In power we are going
In power you come.
(Mu lulendo tweti kwendila
Mu lulendo lwizila.)

When they arrived at the entrance to the village *(fula dia vata),* one of the mwana mbuta who did not make the trip fired a gun to announce both his brothers' successful return and his forefathers' visit. Shortly thereafter the whole community gathered together to welcome them in songs and dances. Each abided by a communal agreement not to sleep so as to avoid angering their guests. To entertain them well the whole night they sang and danced.

In the meantime, the mud the chieftain had brought was deposited at the pulpit of the Protestant church. (The village of Banza-

Lele is overwhelmingly Protestant.) Since each clan-section was to bring its own grave-earth, the pulpit was completely heaped with mud. Then, early the following morning, after the singing and dancing, a cross-shaped pit was dug outside the church. Contrary to usage in the Kibunzi area, where two different crosses were used—a cross-shaped pit symbolizing the cross of Jesus and a wooden one symbolizing the death by nailing to the cross of any ndoki who refused to abandon his kindoki[22]—in the Banza-Lele region there was no wooden cross, only the cross-shaped pit. When the pit was ready, all the mud deposited in the church was taken out and dumped into it. To lighten it, palm wine was poured in again. The Bible was read from, Christian songs were sung, and then the great moment came, namely, kukusa. The first person to take the stand was Duki (Chief) Mabwaka, who represented the village in governmental matters. He cleansed himself by saying:

> As I am chief of this village
> Many suspect me
> As a ndoki.
> Now I am standing in front of this cross.
> You the elders at Makulu are witnesses;
> You brothers here too are witnesses.
> If indeed I am a ndoki,
> If I ate someone,
> Let it be the end.
> Otherwise if I do it again
> My reward will be death.

(For the Kikongo text, see the appendix.)

As he knelt, the supervisor of the rite dipped his hand in the mud to anoint Duki Mabwaka's face so that he received the ancestors' blessing. From that very moment he was under kukusa oath. With the exception of the first line, all those who did kukusa repeated what Chief Mabwaka had said, then dipped their hands in the mud and marked the sign of the cross on their own faces, sealing the oath. If one were to remain innocent of being ndoki, this sign would serve as a blessing; if not, it would work as a self-curse. Regardless of age or gender, each individual was to kukusa. Those who refused became outcasts, unwanted. Children said nothing, but were to stand in front of the cross-pit and place grave-earth mud on their faces. It took the whole day for everyone to kukusa. When it was over, the cross-pit was covered. It remained for several months under the protection of the chief.

The climax of the rite would come in an emotional confession in which a renowned ndoki would publicly denounce his science. The confession is the pragmatic achievement of the Munkukusa rite. It can be interpreted as leading to the psychological and social integration of the whole community. Because of its importance, I will give an example of such a confession as fully as possible. I do not reveal the name of the individual for two reasons: he was my grandfather, and since he is now dead I am bound by tradition to respect him. Accordingly, the pseudonym *tata* (father) Yola is used.

Yola was often suspected of being a harmful ndoki, but since he was pleasant to people in ordinary daily life, it was difficult to confirm this. But he led a double life. While during the day he was one of the nicest men in the village, at night he was one of the ugliest, one of the merciless ones.

According to his own account he became a ndoki by biological inheritance when he was still a fetus in his mother's womb. It was she who wanted him to be a ndoki. She handed on to him bad spirits *(mpeve zambi)* and witchcraft-substance *(kundu)*.[23] Kundu is the invisible organism by means of which a ndoki "eater" accomplishes his work. It is an integral part of his being; without it he cannot do any harm. It is the motive agent of every imaginable evil act caused by kindoki. This belief has been widely observed, as Hallen and Sodipo note in their study of witchcraft: "Witches are sometimes thought to derive certain of their powers from witchcraft substance, either internal to the body of the witch, or kept by her in some external, secret place."[24]

Here is the full account of what tata Yola confessed to the public: "Although kindoki is everywhere, we have a rule limiting our operational zone to blood brotherhood. No ndoki is allowed to operate outside his zone, that is, no ndoki is entitled to attack an unrelated individual. Hence, each ndoki operates in his own circle. This is the rule of kindoki by which we all abide firmly and with good grace. It may however be overruled in case a treaty exists between ndoki of different clan-sections. It must be pointed out that if at any time I want to operate outside my territory, the first step is to gain the approval of an allied ndoki related to my intended victim. Only after an accord has been reached does the door for me open. Any intruder who acts on his own to harm non-kin will be killed by other ndoki. This is the type of protection we provide to our families. It is misleading to believe that we only eat; we protect too. A 'ndoki-less' family will never stand; it will be consumed in a very short time, for no one will protect it." This statement is confirmed by Wyatt MacGaffey's researches in Lower Zaire: "*Kundu* [witchcraft] power is not intrinsically selfish, however; a good magician has to have *kundu* because without it he cannot make the dead appear. Elders must have *kundu dyandundila kanda,* with which they protect the clan."[25]

To continue with tata Yola's confession: "As you know, bandoki love to do things together. This togetherness is vital to avoid unpleasantness and sudden attacks. There may be three or four different associations of bandoki in a single village; mine boasts of ndoki from three different clan-sections. Nevertheless, I have the privilege of not naming them. The unique advantage of these small groups is that they ease our burden; otherwise all the major decisions are taken by all bandoki of neighboring villages engaged in *kitemo*. [*Kitemo* in this case can be described as a commercial association in which each participant brings his own contribution.] In other words, when we intend to 'eat' a specific person we persuade the ndoki of the family concerned to contribute him or her. If they refuse, the matter must be debated, and sometimes it may take weeks or months before a satisfactory solution is found.

"When no family volunteers to provide a victim, we draw lots. Again, this process may take weeks or months. We are very patient. But in general, everything goes smoothly as planned. However, my most frustrating experience as ndoki comes when I have no alternative but to provide my closest relative such as son, daughter, brother, sister, or parent. Doubtless this is the most devastating period for any ndoki. There are those who decline to comply with the demand, but by doing so they endanger their own lives. Therefore we appreciate a ndoki (but by no means do we encourage him) who sacrifices his own life in order to save that of his beloved kin.

"Certainly you are interested to hear how we catch our victims.

When everyone sleeps is the propitious time to operate. Then our soul leaves this physical body and flits out to the intended victim's house. Shortly afterward it has captured the soul and neutralized it. It then returns or joins other ndoki at their headquarters called Kanga dia bandoki. This soul is like our physical body. From the moment of the attack, the victim grows sick until death if the purpose is to 'eat' him. I strongly deny that during this operation we are naked. We are neither naked nor clothed. The body in which we operate has nothing to do with clothing or nakedness. Since my purpose in this confession is to become a 'born again' human being, I would rather prefer to stop here."

Astonished, no one dared to ask him anything more.

His testimony was disappointing in his failure (perhaps it was not his concern) to unveil the mystery behind the fascinating question of how a ndoki is capable of "eating" another human being. But in general it was a revealing and helpful experience. It eased tensions between himself, his closest kin, and the remainder of the family, but it did not diminish the grief they felt about his diabolical activities.

Priests of Divine Science

A fuller insight into the phenomenon of kindoki can be gained by studying the notion of *kinganga.* The two are parallel and interconnected.

In his Kikongo-French dictionary, Karl Laman, a Swedish missionary who studied BaManianga, defines *kinganga* as the usage, customs, manners, quality, and rights pertaining to a pagan medical priest. That is, he understands it to be a pagan priesthood. He is both right and wrong. It is a priesthood, and from a Christian point of view it can be seen as "pagan" science; but from the traditional African point of view, it is not pagan—it is divine. The nganga can be regarded as the bridge between the communities of the dead and the living beings. (The terms *nganga* and *kinganga,* like *ndoki* and *kindoki,* refer respectively to the practitioner and his art. *Bandoki* and *banganga* are plurals.)

Nganga is neither a magician, witch, faker, nor sorcerer; yet he is all of these and much more. As used by BaManianga, the term *nganga* denotes a physician or medical man, pharmacist, prophet, seer, visionary, fortune-teller, priest, and ndoki. He uses his kindoki to provide help rather than harm. It is not inaccurate to call him the good ndoki, or counterwitch, of bandoki. Working closely with an ancestral spirit, he sits above any imaginable kind of human power. He becomes thereby the factotum and guardian of the community secrets. To some degree he lives in a world of his own. He is the last hope to whom the individual and the entire community turn in time of despair. His kindoki is humano-spiritual; he is possessed by a spirit without being a spirit himself. Remaining constantly in touch with the spirit, he connects the two communities.

When a family's nganga is elected chief, he mostly remains inactive in government affairs, consigning political duties to his closest follower, who could be called, in Western terms, vice-president. His religious obligations are far more demanding than his political ones; if he neglects the first he could be in conflict with the spirit, a situation no one wants to be in.

All banganga do not possess the same power and qualifications. There are different classes, and the most important are described in the following discussion.

Ngang'a Ngombo, the Searchers of Causes

Every living thing, every event of fortune or misfortune occurring to particular individuals or the whole community, must be attributed to an origin or cause. Nothing is ever thought of as uncaused. Though fortunate events such as good luck *(nsunzila)* remain inexplicable and are gladly accepted, any unfortunate event must be explained. In case of serious illness or death, for example, when not due to natural old age, the community members bring the case to ngang'a ngombo, the priest who searches causes. In order to obtain a more reliable explanation and result, they usually consult a distant ngang'a ngombo whom they perhaps do not know. The farther away, the better and more acceptable are his findings. A local ngang'a ngombo may take advantage of turmoil within the group to reach his verdict.

Ngombo refers to the fetish, which is the incarnation of the spirit he uses to carry out his divination. It is generally made away from the village. It includes *mpemba* (chalk), *tukula* (something red), and an object or plant recommended by the spirit. Nganga is dressed in leopard skin (the symbol of power) and *mbongo* (traditional bark cloth, a fabric for rich people); he carries a walking-stick and a box in which he keeps all his mysterious objects, especially white ashes believed to be from the dead (*mungw'a basenzi,*[26] literally, "indigenous salt"), palm nuts to launch curses against whoever is the evildoer, raffia threads, *luvemba* (leaves of a plant used for healing), snails, armlets, and many other objects.

After he has collected what he needs, he gathers the consulting family to begin the process of "cause finding." The method he adopts is that of question and answer. There are no idle onlookers; all members are required to be active from the start until the end of the process. They sing, clap hands, and dance. Then, conversing with them, he makes inquiries about the case:

> Nganga: E ma a a (Take!)
> Audience: Vana (Give)
> Nganga: E sweka (Hidden)
> Audience: E solula (Find)
> Nganga: E e malavu (Drink)
> Audience: E e sala ntete (First perform your duty, then you will have your drink.)

This colloquy must be repeated at least three times before nganga moves on to the next phase, which he inaugurates with this song:

> I am going to make ngombo with this chalk
> I am the true nganga
> Let us fight
> Hurry up
> Where is the cause I will miss?
> I am the nganga . . .
> (E mu luvemba yatela ngombo e wawa ee wawaa
> Mono nganga e wawa ee wawaa
> Twakakaseno e wawa ee wawaa
> Kuma ntangu ee
> Kwe diabwila yazimbwe?
> Mono nganga eee . . .)[27]

As he falls into ecstasy, the audience designates a very wise man to challenge the nganga's reliability by asking him: "Why have we consulted you? What have we lost?" (Nkia bila tukutombele? Nki tuvidisi?). The nganga ignores the question and continues to sing: "Kwe diabwila yazimbwe e?" Then, softly but firmly, he responds, "You have consulted me not because you have lost something; you have consulted me because one of you is near death." Aloud, he then asks himself, "Are you sleeping, nganga?" (Nganga lele e?).

> Audience: Proceed with your speech. (E le e le mama.)
> Wise man: Is the patient a man or a woman? (Nga mbevo yabakala evo yankento?)
> Nganga: A man (or a woman, as the case may be).

Saying this, he denounces the family to which the culprit responsible for the illness presumably belongs.

In the meantime, the innocent family (paternal or maternal) exults: "Oh, oh, you endlessly give no end of trouble to us, now who is right? Can you talk big again? Stop bewitching. Let the [little] children grow up peacefully." (Oh, oh, lelo kamba beto, ka lumweni ko? Luvova diaka bwabu? Luyambula kindoki kieno. Luyambula biabana biakula.)

Then he proceeds to the greatest challenge of all, the isolation of the suspected ndoki. Before denouncing him or her, nganga is entranced. His eyes become almost red, he speaks in an unintelligible language no one understands. It is believed that at this particular moment he is a man of two worlds. He is taken into the other world to confront his spirit, his *nkisi*. He remains in ecstasy until an agreement is reached as to who the ndoki is. As he emerges from the other world, he unhesitatingly accuses him or her. It is a surprise if the accused individual is not an elder. With this, his task as ngang'a ngombo ends. He may recommend the patient to a particular *ngang'a mbuki,* or healer.

Ngang'a Mbuki, the Healers

Ngang'a mbuki, or ngang'a nkisi as most people prefer to call him, is the physician or medicine man who cures both physical and spiritual diseases. He organizes one or more meetings at which he gives himself up to dance, ecstasy, and all kinds of gestures, setting himself up as an indispensable and powerful person.

He openly uses his nkisi, or spirit, materialized into *futu,* a small bag containing several objects more or less whimsical. For nkisi cannot participate in the healing process without the material support of futu. The indigenous medicine or herb the nganga prescribes to his patient must have been recommended by nkisi; otherwise it will do no good.

Sometimes he prescribes nothing to the patient but goes to the root, namely, the bewitching person, so that nkisi, or spirit-force, can either neutralize or kill him. As Konda Jean told Laman, "The nganga may bury nkisi medicines at the entrances to the village. When a witch crosses them the nkisi goes after him, but if an innocent person (muntu wa nana) without any witchcraft crosses them the nkisi will not follow him."[28] To succeed in his profession, the nganga must scrupulously follow nkisi's instructions; if he does not, the nkisi will be angered and even turn against him. Nkisi is the provider and nganga the "spirit carrier." In other words, he is nkisi's servant.

In 1972, as I was investigating Kongo-Manianga religion for my *mémoire de licence* at the University of Zaire, I had the privilege of talking with my older half-brother, Philemon. Before converting to Christianity he had been a famed ngang'a nkisi. Because of this reputation his own community frequently suspected him of being an "eater" of others' souls. His life was sometimes threatened, but he could not give up a profession he loved so much. In becoming Christian he closed the door to his "pagan" past life. He never wished to discuss it with anyone. Surprisingly, then, he was more than cooperative in responding to my inquiries. Here is how our conversation went:

> Q: When and how did you become nganga?
> A: First and foremost, I must tell you that I was not nganga. I was mbuki (healer). I do not recall when I started curing because as you know we do not put much interest in chronology of events; I was probably less than twenty-five years old. As to the second part of your question, I was recommended to heal the sick in a dream.
> Q: You did not learn it at Kinkimba? [Kinkimba, a kind of school, will be discussed below.]

A: No. I never attended that school. As a matter of fact, in my days Kinkimba was already a thing of the past.

Q: How did you come to know the right medicine to use for a particular disease and patient?

A: I often dreamed it. My ancestors, chiefly *nkaka* Bayengika [our grandmother], were always with me. At night when I was asleep they not only revealed to me the names of *minti* [herbs and plants] to use, they also showed me how to use them. This is the main reason why I hardly ever experienced failure in my career. I was well equipped.

Q: Can you tell me some of the minti you often dreamed?

A: I cannot recall all, but some are *munsangula* to cure *kinsiala* [chronic diarrhea and toothache]; *kinseka* to cure skin disease; *nsa* to soften cough; *nlulukulu* to relieve stomach ache due to poisonous food; *kimbanzia* to defend or protect someone from something or someone else; *nkusa-nkusa* to fight ulcer.

Q: How did you handle an emergency? Did you wait first for an ancestor to tell you what to do?

A: No, I could not wait for their participation. I only used my personal knowledge. I also got some help from uncle Wamba, who himself was strong in healing. [He is now dead.]

Q: Did you like this profession?

A: Fighting bad spirits in order to save someone's life high-spirited me. It made me aware of being somebody.

Q: Then why did you give it up?

A: I did not give it up. I was called to be Jesus' servant. [His fundamentalist spiritual group refuses to recognize the validity of traditional Kongo religion.]

Q: Any regrets?

A: Yes, for I lost my close ties with the ancestors. No, for I feel much happier to be associated with Jesus.

The main distinction between nganga and ndoki is that while most nganga (but by no means all) possess both ndoki and nkisi, ndoki has no nkisi, or benevolent spirit. Because of this, they see one another as adversaries rather than friends or colleagues.

Training in the Science of Kinganga

Because of the important role nganga play in Kongo society, it is vital to understand how one is initiated into kinganga, the mysterious science of dealing with life on two levels. Today, any persons whom the ancestors elect can become nganga by either a dream or by direct initiation from another nganga chosen by the family's ancestors. But in the past it was different. To become nganga one had to attend a local traditional school called Kinkimba (or, in other parts of Manianga, Kimpasi, literally, "suffering"). The chief concern of this school was the complete formation of the individual as a human being. The importance it had in those days can be compared with the importance of a university today. A country without a university and university graduates is considered backward or worthless; similarly, a community with no Kinkimba graduate was not well respected. For example, in Manianga today we recognize two kinds of families or communities; those with university graduates are "first class," and those which have none are "second class." The same could have been said about Kinkimba.

Generally, four fields were taught. In the first, law *(kinzonzi),* the students were taught to become good judges *(nzonzi),* advocates, and guardians of the ancestors' land. They learned how to argue and speak well. They studied tradition *(kinkulu),* enigma, proverbs, and *bunseki* (from *nseki,* which Laman defines as "the person who begins, who leads off with a song, a tune; director of a song; composer of a song.")[29] Musicality is an indispensable tool for a nzonzi. A nzonzi who does not know how to sing cannot preside over a Manianga marriage ceremony. He must be a good singer and dancer to claim his salary for whatever he is to do for his host family.

The second field, medicine and pharmacy *(kinganga kia buka),* represented by my brother's work, has been described above.

In the third field, tradition and history *(kinkulu),* students studied the history of Kongo-Manianga roots, migration, and the tradition of the major clan. After graduation they became teachers of their particular tradition to their communal brothers who were not so fortunate as to attend Kinkimba.

The fourth field, *kinganga kia ngombo,* encompassed religion, psychology, parapsychology, and philosophy.

Besides his field of specialization, each student had to take general courses to make him a complete being. Some of the general training dealt with how to be brave and wise in order to protect the family or any other person against enemies; how to endure sufferings and others' teasings (for example, when a student made a mistake, he was to be scourged; however, he was not allowed to cry or pull a long face; he was to be happy all the time); how to handle emergencies; how to be a decent individual; and how to master Kinkimba language so that when members of the community talked, no neophyte could follow the conversation at a distance (whoever failed to speak it fluently could not graduate).

The teachers were called *mabaku* and the students *nkimba*. Fathers who sent sons to this school were obligated to build their sons' huts *(mafwokula)*. It is not clear whether they also built the teachers' huts. The site where the school was built was called *nlemba,* or *vwala*. It was holy as long as the school stood there. Any outsider was by law forbidden to loiter around.

Generally the school was for young unmarried men, but sometimes married individuals willing to obey the teachers and the school rules were admitted. A family with no Kinkimba graduate was a mere mockery. Girls were never part of the school. Nevertheless, since the tradition exhorts men not to cook their own meals, good housewives were hired to cook at the Kinkimba. They were called *malambi,* "cookers." They thereby became part of the school and to some extent even became students of the school. In this way many of them picked up fluency in Kinkimba language. These women learned much from students' conversations and as a result rose from being "second" to being "first" class members of their families. Very often men who had not attended Kinkimba sought their advice.

The initiation rite of Kinkimba was carried out according to a fourfold pattern consisting of selection, separation, transition, and reunion. Separated from the others and locked up, the initiate experienced a personal life crisis. Beth Elverdam describes this kind of initiation:

> The novices are brought into a world which has no connections with ordinary life. Often they are considered as non-existent and regarded as dead or embryos. In this way they are trapped in a situation in which there is little or no possibility for them to return

to the ordinary world before the rite is over and they are reborn
through the incorporation rite. They are psychologically under
stress and in this connection one might postulate that their per-
ceptive mechanisms are raised to a more acute level of
sensitivity.[30]

This is true also of Kinkimba. Benjamin C. Ray adds:

> At this critical period people are neither what they were nor what
> they will become. Initiates are neither children nor adults, male
> nor female, human nor animal. They are momentary anomalies,
> stripped of their former mode of being, ready to become some-
> thing new. Similarly, the time between the seasons and the time
> between the years belongs neither to the old nor the new, but to
> both. It is a time out of time, when the usual order of things is
> reversed and thrown back to primordial chaos, ready to become
> reestablished and renewed in a new order of temporality.[31]

The exit from one stage of life to the next, that is, from baby-
hood to ancestorhood, is marked by death and rebirth. Consequently, death is never portrayed as the end. Although every
"life-exit" requires symbolic death, the pain the initiate goes
through is experienced differently by each individual. Doubtless
the Kinkimba rite was the climax of every imaginable suffering
and joy.

The length of schooling varied from two to four years. Owing to
the lack of a dating system, schooling was numbered by seasons.
Throughout his attendance at the school, each initiate was to
comply with the school rules. Once having entered, the student
was not permitted to return home until the rite[32] or school was
over. He was to comply with all teachers' orders. Any reluctance
might be punished severely. Living at a holy site, the student was
ipso facto holy. He was not supposed to be seen by an uninitiated
person (mungwala).[33] Anyone who was caught having gone to
the village and in the act of performing sex, even with his own
wife, was executed without mercy; otherwise his defilement
would contaminate the school's purity and holiness. According to
Reverend Bahalele,[34] in other parts of Manianga such an individual was buried alive by his own community to show its
disapproval of his not living up to its expectations.

As one might expect, the most time was devoted to the training of banganga in the secret knowledge of two different worlds: the visible world of human beings and the invisible world of spirits. Not only did they learn how to protect the society against evil, or kindoki kia dia, they also learned how to behave vis-à-vis the spirits. They were even invited to initiate themselves with nkisi of their choice.

The acquisition of all such knowledge, as might be supposed, was a one-way communication. Students could neither doubt nor ask questions. Upon graduation, they became the most important members of the society. What they accomplished for their communities may be compared with what the academic world is accomplishing today in other ways.

Education of young people in the traditions and ways of the community, even without any kind of formal schooling, still persists in family groups. Men gather after work in the shelterhouse to relax and talk. Their discussions are not merely of events of the day or happenings in the village. The oldest man, who is often the family leader as well, leads the talk, which dwells on family history, going as far back as possible. He talks of where the people came from, the fields they work, the forests they have, notable incidents in their history. Others who are close to him in age chime in, adding what he may not remember. Small boys listen respectfully; teenagers are taught more directly and may ask questions. They are not required to start attending these sessions at the early age of five, but many do, pushed by their mothers. The groups also discuss family principles and beliefs. For example, my family has strongly believed in the principle that a child should never be beaten. This was because many generations ago a child died as the result of a beating, and it was determined that no child should ever again be so treated.

By the age of twenty-five a man will know his entire family history, which he will carry in his head wherever he may go. Even if he leaves home to work elsewhere, he will return from time to time and hear it again when the elders gather almost every day to talk. Nowadays a family member will often act as a kind of secretary and make written records of the family story.

Since men work in their fields alone much of the time and in groups only to accomplish particular tasks, these meetings are important for knitting family bonds. Women, on the other hand, work together in their fields and bring the girls of all ages with them. Their talk of family takes place as they work together. The smallest boys remain in the village and play together, supervised by old men and women who can no longer work; these boys also help those who are too feeble to care for themselves. Then, if they are not too small, they meet with the men in the shelterhouse when they return from work.

A New Type of Priesthood: Kingunza

Many Christians, as we have seen, continue to rely privately on traditional priest-healers (nganga) despite the effort by Western-based churches to suppress them. But for Christians who feel driven to resolve the conflict between two religions, both of which they feel committed to, new syncretic, independent churches or religious movements have sprung up in both the villages and the larger cities. These movements have created a new category of priesthood known as *kingunza.*

The new priest, or *ngunza,* functions essentially like the traditional nganga described above. But unlike nganga, who depends on the guidance of the ancestors, ngunza depends on the Holy Spirit. People come to him, just as to nganga, to seek blessings or help in misfortune. But instead of specializing in one particular kind of service, such as healing, searching causes, or solving problems, ngunza encompasses them all.

Since illness continues to be attributed to bad spirits, ngunza's role is to expel them. A sick person may be brought to a meeting of the group, often an outdoor area, where people sometimes sit on rows of benches in an enclosed yard. Or they may meet in the leader's house, if there is room. A church building is not considered necessary, since God is held to be everywhere and cannot be confined to a particular space. Some groups, in fact, do not believe in meeting indoors at all.

The rituals, a blend of various Christian and native traditions, vary considerably from one group to another, for they tend to work out their own original approaches. The elders of the church—*prophètes*—pray, sprinkle holy water, or swish towels to chase the evil spirits away. Confession, which we have seen to be a key element in traditional rituals of cleansing and reconciliation, has assumed even greater importance in many independent churches. To head off communal or family misfortune, members can go to ngunza daily to confess sins, thereby making themselves able to begin each new day as a cleansed person. Traditionally, mass confession was used only after a crisis had been reached, when the buildup of "sins" in the group had led to an explosion requiring each person to confess his or her part. In kingunza, individuals confess their sins daily as a way of preventing such a buildup over a period of time. This idea of daily confession was doubtless borrowed from the Catholic Church.

Ngunza, like nganga, must be in touch with the world of spirit. He does this through the exercise of psychic perception and receiving messages in dreams. My half-brother Philemon is such a *prophète,* and is in much demand. Spiritual messages, however, are not delivered on the spot as they are in Western spiritualist churches, or by Western-style psychics, who seem to be involved most commonly in a kind of business enterprise. One may ask ngunza questions, but the answer usually comes later, for the spirit chooses when and how to give.

In the larger cities, kingunza provides an opportunity for people with a wide variety of backgrounds to participate together, because the Holy Spirit offers a kind of universality, as contrasted to the specific ancestors of a village group. It is a useful adaptation to the otherwise disintegrative forces of modern urban life. But independent churches thrive as well in the villages, where they may be tied to a single community or to a group of neighboring villages. The flexibility of kingunza allows it to flourish everywhere.

Unknown to the conventional Christian churches, groups of their regular members sometimes meet privately with ngunza, rotating their meetings among their homes. In the 1960s many were expelled from their churches when they were found out. Harassed by the churches and disillusioned that they were not receiving the spiritual help they desired, many have left voluntarily to found their own independent churches.

Perhaps the first, and most famous, of the independent churches is Kimbanguism. Its origin is described by Mahaniah Kimpianga:

Modern *prophetisme* in most of the Kongo areas has for origin the appearance of Simon Kimbangu. April 6, 1921 Kimbangu from Nkamba village in Bas-Zaire cured a dying woman and became known instantly as a prophet by the whole population of the Belgian Congo (today Zaire). September 12, 1921 Kimbangu was arrested and sent to the central prison of Elizabethville (today Lubumbashi). Kimbangu died after 30 years of imprisonment. Recognized as *nganga* [before being jailed], Kimbangu was being visited by people from Bas-Zaire in hope of resurrecting the dead, healing the sick, blessing by laying on of hands in order to protect them from all kinds of diseases and witchcraft. Let us note that the people of Belgian Congo, in particular in Lower Zaire, were impatiently awaiting a redeemer to save them from the rupture of the traditional structure of their lives.[35]

Kimbanguism is an exception to some of the above comments about independent churches, in that it is a widespread organization, not limited to one local or ethnic group centering on a particular ngunza. Its main headquarters is in Kimbangu's village, Nkamba, which, like Mecca, has become a center for pilgrimages.

The close political association of the Christian churches with colonial rule is evident in the suppression of Kimbanguism and the explosive growth of new churches with a revival of interest in traditional beliefs following independence. To many, Christianity is acceptable only when it can be reconciled with traditional beliefs. An example can be seen in Kimbanguism's adaptation of an element of Christian ritual, "In the name of God, Christ, the Holy Spirit, and Simon Kimbangu," thus adding the idea of ancestors to the Holy Trinity.

There may be a subtler and deeper significance in this as well. Carl Jung has argued that a trinity is an incomplete symbol; universally, a group of four, or a quaternary, has represented completeness and can be found in religions worldwide.[36] By adding the human element to the divine, Kimbanguism in effect not only blends Christian and African traditions, but restores spiritual completeness.

Individuals caught in the crosscurrents of religious conflict sometimes go through periods of tumultuous inner upheaval before reaching an acceptable balance among the influences to which they are subjected. An interesting case is that of a man I knew in Kinshasa, Masala Dominique, originally from Kingoyi area, district of Mongo Luala.

I came to know tata Dominique at the choir in a church I attended. After choir practice he often took me to the bakery where he worked to give me free bread. He was married and had one daughter, and both he and his wife were devoted Christians. Despite our friendship I did not know the real tata Dominique until perhaps two years later. Besides being a member of our choir, he was a deacon and *nlongi* (teacher) in an underground religious sect. Contrary to most ngunza movements, this was a movement of fundamentalist Christians who were also members of a missionary church. But being members of the church did not mean accepting 100 percent of its teaching. They rejected any teaching that did not fit their religious beliefs. They were so conservative they accepted literally everything the Bible says, refusing to believe that the New Testament is the fulfillment of the Old Testament. Daily confession of sins was strictly required. It reads in part: "In the name of the Father, Son, and Holy Spirit I kneel before you the apostles of Jesus to confess any wrongdoing I have done today. Forgive me so that my heart may be clean as snow." (For the Kikingo text, see the appendix.)

Members of this sect were expected to live like monks; secularism was their number one enemy. But this did not mean that they rejected their traditional values. Despite the purity they aspired to, a mixture of Christian and traditional beliefs existed among them. Most of the time they kept themselves separate from the rest of society, but when important events occurred, such as a death, a marriage, or restoration of a broken covenant with ancestors, they were not only involved but observed all the required rites. When an inexplicable death within a community required consultation with a nganga, members of this sect did not object. They attended, even though they considered themselves to be more powerful than banganga.

After becoming acquainted with the real tata Dominique, I (being young and full of questions) wanted to know why he became a member of that religious community. This is what he told me.

As a youth he had attended a Catholic elementary school in Mongo Luala. After graduation he moved to Matadi, the largest city in Lower Zaire and Zaire's seaport, the "city of milk and honey." About a month after he arrived, he found a job and was making good money. He regularly attended mass for about a year, but after being immersed in the permissive atmosphere of the city, he said goodbye to mass and the church. Thereafter he became a heavy drinker and went to bed with all kinds of women. Being alcoholic and "oversexual," he grew so careless of his work that he finally lost his job.

Then one night, sitting in his tiny, half-lighted apartment, he began to see what he called "spiritual lights"—blue, yellow, red, and white. Frightened, he ran into the streets, but this unexplainable mystery would not let him escape. Exhausted, he fell to the ground. Then he heard a soft voice: "Dominique, stand up. Go to Bikuta Axel. Tell him what you saw." It was his first time to hear the name of Bikuta Axel, and he was even more frightened and confused. He had no idea who the man was who had spoken to him, nor did he know where to find this Bikuta Axel.

For two days he confined himself to his apartment, not knowing what to do. In the meantime, a close friend was so worried that he went to see him. After Dominique told his story, the friend took him to another friend, a churchgoer, to find out about Bikuta Axel. This friend knew Bikuta Axel and gave them his home address. Bikuta Axel was the national leader of a prophetic movement.

Tata Dominique hurried to Bikuta's house to tell him his vision. The interpretation he received was that God was calling Dominique to the ministry. He joined Bikuta's prophetic movement and was converted to Protestantism. He was happy to be able to put his life together again. He found a job and a year later married a young woman who was also a member of the movement. All of his spare time was devoted to religious activities: worship, prayer meetings in private homes, and Bible reading.

On the eve of the political independence of Zaire, the company he worked for was closed. Unemployed, he persuaded his wife to move to Kinshasa. They settled in Kintambo, where they joined another group within the same movement. A few weeks later he found a job paying so well that he bought a motorcycle and a portion of land on which to build his own house. Despite his material success, he remained completely devoted to the church, the movement, and his clan-section. He did so in order to avoid any repetition of his mistakes of the past.

As a friend, he constantly urged me to join the movement, but to no avail. Later he became critical of my own belief, which he said he could not understand. I was a member of a church and choir he approved of, but as long as I refused to join his movement also, in his mind I was not yet saved. Despite our religious differences, we remained good friends. Any time I was in need he did not hesitate to help me. When I went away to the university we continued to correspond for a year.

Tata Dominique was so indoctrinated by Christian teachings that he had no time to examine himself about what he was being taught. He accepted everything without question or doubt. Then in 1971 he met a friend who was studying anthropology at the National University of Zaire, Kinshasa. They became good friends and saw each other regularly. In spite of having attended Protestant elementary and high schools, this friend did not consider himself a Christian. He said that before going to the university he also was brainwashed and accepted Christianity as the only road to salvation, "but after I became a student of anthropology, I began to understand the importance of one's own culture. Consequently, I questioned the teaching of the missionaries and their condemnation of my culture."

After hearing this, and because of the respect he had for his university friend, tata Dominique became so disillusioned about his new faith that he suffered a psychotic breakdown. Since he did not have a good education, he could not think his way through to a resolution of his conflict. He became withdrawn, critical of Christianity, the sect, and even Jesus Christ. He no longer believed that he could not be saved outside the church. The only remaining thing to do, then, was to return to his traditional beliefs. To make public his departure from the church and the prophetic movement, he married a second wife, becoming polygamous, an intolerable sin in the eyes of church teaching. Unless some unexpected event happens to him again, he has no intention of rejoining either the church or his former sect.

Similar cases can be found in almost every corner of Manianga. Those who begin to question the missionary teachings and intent may break irrevocably with them and return to their familiar saviors: the ancestors. Returning to traditional beliefs after a temporary lapse, they often become the most conservative traditionalists, because they want to make up quickly for whatever damage their conversion to Christianity and neglect of traditional values may have done to the community and the kanda.

An Overview of Kindoki

Kindoki has been viewed by outsiders—and by many Westernized Africans—as the survival of a "primitive" superstition that stands in the way of progress and the development of Manianga society. But after becoming engaged in this study, I have come to regard it as a complex system of social checks and balances that works for the health and wholeness, the preservation and continuance, of the community, capable of providing opportunities for wealth, power, knowledge, and dedication to the common good while controlling the disruptive factors of anger, vengeance, and violence. Seen in this light, kindoki is a subtle cultural science that serves a vital function. It is an impressive social achievement that cannot be easily abandoned. So deep are its roots, it is likely to survive in adapted forms in the course of social development.

III

THE CONCEPT OF DEATH

Death as an Opening to a Better or a Worse Life

The traditional Manianga explanation of death is that to die does not mean to be finished, to vanish or decompose. Rather, in dying one gets the opportunity for a better life if one has lived according to social norms and expectations, or for a worse life if one has not.[?] Death is defined primarily as a departure, a change. To die is to leave the visible world for the invisible; it is to say no to hunger, misery, disease, and worry. It is to say goodbye to the earth. Mujynya, who has studied the Banyarwanda people of Rwanda, finds a similar idea when he writes of the person who has died: "He has left, he has gone back, he has preceded us to the home of our elders 'the ancestors,' he has said goodbye to the earth . . ."[1]

This departure, however, is not an eternal separation. From time to time the deceased return home to warn, inform, or give instructions to the kanda or an individual member regarding an upcoming event looming large *(lwengisa),* or to reprimand or punish *(semba).* The departed are also impelled to return when there is an important event such as a marriage, *matanga* (a rite honoring the dead), or a dispute between two clan-sections. When the deceased feel neglected by the living, they have a sanctioned right to let their displeasure be known, to punish or blame the person who is the cause of their neglect. They may also punish the whole kanda; that is, the welfare of everyone, the fertility of the soil, may be damaged.

The kind of life the dying person is to lead in the next world is a reflection of the life he or she has lived on earth. A good man is believed to go to Mpemba, the ancestors' world, a world without hunger, thirst, disease, or feud. It is a world where one enjoys the

83

benefits of one's goodness on earth. Admission into this world is not based on the criterion of having an irreproachable faith in God but rather on how the dying person has carried out the ancestors' orders, and what he or she has done to assure the welfare of each member of the kanda. Those who are communalists are assured of reaching Mpemba. But those who have centered their lives on selfishness are excluded regardless of their social status. The following case is an illustration of how a former leader of a kanda was rejected and not allowed to enter Mpemba.

Mayu (a pseudonym), the leader of Kingoyi clan-section in the village of Banza-Lele, district of Kivunda, was a famed ndoki. Instead of working for the welfare of the whole family, he devoted himself to hurting those kin who struggled to better their own lives and that of the entire kanda. If a member was too successful in whatever he was doing, Mayu put a stop to his efforts by "eating" him. He hated everybody, even his own children.

In the summer of 1969, one of his mwana mbuta (child of the male lineage) who was studying in Kinshasa went home to visit his maternal uncle, who was hospitalized at Mangembo with a broken leg. Because the hospital had no visitors' rooms, he commuted on foot for two weeks between Mangembo and the village, a round trip each day of about sixty kilometers. Finally, exhausted and worn out, he decided to return to Kinshasa and escape the difficult country life. But as required by custom, he could not leave without notice. He was first urged by his mother to seek a blessing from his paternal ancestors through their representative, the living chief—who was Mayu.

In this case, however, Chief Mayu, who had hated this mwana mbuta's father very much during his lifetime, was to take advantage of this opportunity to curse rather than bless the innocent boy. Usually the ceremony takes place during the day and in front of the paternal kanda. Instead, Mayu held it at night in a dark room of his house without witnesses. Mayu addressed his brother's son in a trembling voice, for he knew that he was not saying the truth. The boy who was being "blessed," knowing nothing of the real intent, kept replying yobo ("let it be as you said") to everything his uncle was reciting. After speaking, Mayu handed him a five-franc bill so old that the letters were almost all erased. The purpose of giving him this money was to mysteriously disorient him, so that he would never prosper in anything he undertook. Even small matters or problems would become too difficult to handle. Instead of being blessed the boy was being cursed without his knowledge. Mayu's intention was to render him stupid.

But as BaManianga say, "At Mpemba is one of yours who will assist you in time of trouble" (Ku Mpemba kwatekila wa waku ukudila mvutu). On the eve of his departure, his dead father visited the boy's oldest sister in a dream. He explained to her the purpose of Mayu's "blessing" and how to get rid of it. He ordered his daughter to have her little brother throw away the five-franc bill and to assure him that his father would accompany him safely back to Kinshasa. Without this intervention by his father, the boy would almost certainly be dead today. Even so, his touching of the evil money and Mayu's ceremonial application of saliva to the boy's upraised palms, which he then wiped on his body to signify receiving the blessing, ensured that the false blessing would have some disastrous effects on his life. For three years he had unaccountable fits of giddiness. Again his father came to his rescue in a dream. He ordered him to see *tata* Mwanda, a prophet-healer, who was a general in the Zaire army, and have Mwanda pray for him. *Tata* Mwanda did so for three days, and after that his fits of giddiness left him completely. Mayu remained on watch for his death, only to be disappointed because the boy did not fall into his trap.

Mayu had done similar things to many others. On the day of his death there was no eulogy but rather thanks. He was neither buried as a chief nor lamented. The living community set the tone for his after-death suffering. Since he was at odds with the two communities, visible and invisible, he was rejected by both. The ancestors prohibited him from joining them, for he was unfit to enjoy the benefits of living at Mpemba. Surprised and confused, he began to return to the village. His spirit was often seen wandering around his house. His frightened and shaken kin turned to their last resort: they expelled him definitively from the kanda. Pineapple trees were planted over his grave. For some unknown reason, the evil departed fear to cross over pineapple thorns. Since then he has not been seen again.

Brief Visits to the Unknown (Near-Death Experiences)

As soon as death occurs, the deceased begin their journey to the unknown. Three cases throw light on the nature of this other world.

The first case concerns tata Bethuel, whom I met in July 1964. (*Tata* is a term of affectionate respect not only for one's father but also for any man of the father's generation who is highly respected; I called Bethuel tata because, as my best friend, he was almost of that generation.) The Evangelical Church of Manianga and Matadi (today the Communauté Evangélique du Zaire) had just been established in Kinshasa, and there was a great need for a choir in Bandalungwa, a middle-class section of the city. In 1964 my paternal uncle, Alphonse Batomene, a good singer and composer of religious songs, was invited to form such a choir. He asked me to join it. Though I was preoccupied with my studies and less than enthusiastic, I could never say no to my own uncle, so I enrolled in the choir and was elected its secretary. Two weeks later, tata Bethuel and his son and four nephews joined. At the age of about fifty, he was the oldest and wisest (traditionally speaking) member of the group. And to take full advantage of his seniority, we elected him president.

Being the two top administrative members of the choir, we had frequent business to discuss, and gradually became very close. Each night he invited me to his house. Finally, I became an integral part of his family. To me he was more than just a friend. Although he had a large family and was poor, he gave me everything he thought I might need or want that he could afford. We became so dependent on each other's company that we sometimes stayed in the streets until 2:00 or 3:00 A.M. talking about the spiritual questions that interested us. He was also psychic. Because of our close association, people began to call us "left and right hands." The right hand without getting help from the left hand could not accomplish anything, and reciprocally the left hand could not do anything without the right. This is how we looked at each other.

But despite our closeness, he shied away from telling me that prior to our meeting, he had died briefly. Once, however, he had a severe stomach ache which kept him in bed for several days so that he began to feel concern about his survival. He then spoke freely about death and what I should do in case he did not survive. I was annoyed and worried to hear the same words every day, and decided to ask him why he kept talking about death. At first he laughed and then said, "You are still acting like a child; you do not know that I may indeed die at any moment, even when I am in good health." Thus began the conversation which led to the revelation of his first experience of death.[2]

"I want to hear more about what you just said, because it is beyond my understanding," I told tata Bethuel. "Can you please be specific to your 'left hand'?"

"Sorry, I cannot tell you," tata Bethuel answered.

"Why?"

"Simply because it is beyond your understanding. You will never accept my story."

"If you refuse to tell me, you do not love me as you claim."

"You know that I love you. However, since you begin to have doubts about me, I will have to tell you everything. I have been with you for a few years but this is the first time to reveal to you why I am so concerned about my death, your death, my children's and other loved ones' death. I always think about my next life [the word he used literally means "home"] to avoid being surprised again. I am to be ready every moment, for you do not know the time of your departure. Death is a frightening event when you see it coming. However, if you are prepared to face it, there is no reason to be afraid. Does this make sense to you?"

"Not quite. What do you mean by 'being surprised again'?" Silence. "Tell me, please."

"I do not want to be surprised again as I was during my first death. Are you satisfied?"

"First death? Have you died before?"

"You do not know that all these years you have been dealing with a dead man?" Tata Bethuel's expression was jocular.

"Can you tell me how and when you died?"

"A year before I met you. I was very sick. I knew that I was dying but I was so worried about many things that finally I did not know how to face it. I was really scared. Fortunately, the time my soul made its final exit from the physical body I was unaware. All I do remember is that I was in great pain. My whole body was hurting. Suddenly, I was relieved. I felt no pain. I cannot tell you what happened between pain and relief because I do not know. I can only say that the way I felt at that very moment can be compared to a man who all in a sweat finds himself in a cool place. The air-conditioning cools him off so that he feels just great. This is the way I felt at the time of my death. And because of this great feeling I gave myself to this unexpected anodyne (if I may use the medical term here). I enjoyed every moment of it, not being aware, however, that I was starting my journey to the unknown. I cannot speak for others, but as for me the transition from this life to the next was smooth."

"Did you see anything where you went?"

"As I already said, I do not know the time I left this world. According to what I was told by my 'mourners,' I stopped breathing around 9:00 in the morning and began breathing again around 4:00 or 5:00 in the afternoon. In the meantime I was going somewhere but had no idea of my final destination. I was walking very fast. I saw different things: mountains, trees, grass, palm trees, and people all over the road who were going in the same direction I was going. I saw nobody returning from where we were going. Some were just sitting by the side of the road not knowing what to do. Others were still hanging on at a snail's pace; they were very tired but could not get help from anyone. Everyone was concerned with his own situation. There was no sympathy for others.

"As I was physically strong, I kept speeding up. The men and women I saw were ordinary people. It was a very long journey. Finally, I arrived at a summitless mountain, that is, a huge mountain reaching up beyond human sight or estimation. Hundreds of people were just lying down there because they did not know what to do next. Suddenly, I became depressed myself, but a moment later the name of Jesus Christ came to my mind. Without wasting time, I cried out lustily: 'Jesus, help me!'[3]

"With his help I jumped over the top of the mountain and surprisingly found myself in front of a group of individuals who had *nkanda wamoyo,* the book of life. To be admitted to that world, the name must be found in that huge book. Before being allowed to pass, the name must first be checked and even when it is written in the book, they are to be sure that indeed the individual's time to go there has come. They speak to everyone in his mother tongue. I was amazed to be asked in Kikongo with a Kingoyi accent, 'Nki wizidi?' (Why are you here?) [Tata Bethuel was originally from the Kingoyi area, district of Mongo-Luala.] I honestly said that I did not know how I got there. My whole body was hurting and suddenly it cooled off and I saw myself in the road which had led me to this place.

"They checked my name in nkanda wamoyo. It was there but, unexpectedly, they told me that though my name was there it was not my time to go. They suggested that I return where I came from, but I was less than enthusiastic about their idea. My reluctance was perhaps due to the fact that I did not have enough strength to walk back the same distance. Just as I was having second thoughts, one of them said, 'Tala mwan' aku Marie telamane yandi mosi mukutomba' (Look, your daughter Mary is standing helplessly alone looking for you). She was just one year old. Turning my head to see my daughter, I suddenly found myself back in the middle of a weeping crowd. Completely surprised, I wanted to ask them why they were wailing, but could not. I was unable to open my mouth as it was so dry with no saliva in it. I made a sign that I wanted to say something. They gave me a paper and pen to write. This is what I wrote: Nzolele vova kansi nwa ka weti zibuka ko kadi watoma yuma wena (I want to speak but my mouth is so dry).

"Then they gave me something sweet to loosen my mouth. However, to put it in required some doing. It took a great deal of time before they succeeded."

"Then what happened?"

"My mouth was open. I told them that contrary to what they thought, I was not dead but had gone somewhere I did not myself know. They were incredibly amazed and awed. Those sitting by the bedside began to move quickly away from me. It took them hours to accept me again as a member of the living community."

"Were you disappointed by the way they reacted to your return? In other words, did you think that they were unhappy about your return to this life?"

"Not at all. Their reaction was quite understandable and acceptable. I would do the same thing myself. With the exception of some bandoki, you will never find anyone who is willing to associate or be in the same company with the dead. As you know, we encourage and indeed invite our ancestors to be actively involved in our day-to-day affairs. But despite this close association no one wants to meet his ancestors face to face. Consequently, their reaction was natural."

As he had wished, tata Bethuel was more prepared for his second and final departure. Two days before he died in 1969, he told his elder son that he was departing from this world, though he did not tell the day or time. He washed the clothes he wanted to wear on the day of his death, including a shirt of mine that I had left with him. Unfortunately, as he was not sick, no one took him seriously. I was at the National University of Zaire at Kisangani, over seven hundred miles away, and since I could not physically participate in the process of his departure, the day he died he sent me his last letter. Earlier, he had urged me to try to come home during the brief Christmas break, hinting that it might be the last time we would see each other. But the air flights were too expensive for me to consider it, and besides I did not want to think about the possibility that he might die. His letter was written and mailed early in the morning. At 4:25 that afternoon he collapsed and fell down while at work, and that was the end. By the time they had rushed him to the hospital, he was gone. In his letter he wished me good luck in whatever plans I had for the future and expressed his disappointment that I could not bury him. He also assured me that he would always be around to help me. The last part of his letter was a quotation from the Bible (Joshua 1:8): "This book of the law shall not depart out of your mouth, but you shall meditate on it day and night, that you may be careful to do according to all that is written in it; for then shall you make your way prosperous, and then you shall have good success." BaManianga believe strongly that when an individual is about to die, whether by natural, accidental, or evil causes, he will somehow be informed days or even months before it actually happens. In the case of tata Bethuel's second death, it was revealed to a woman from Sundi-Lutete, who at the time was living in Kinshasa. She knew tata Bethuel well. In the summer of 1967 she dreamed of being told that a very important member of her

church would die. And then his name was given—tata Bethuel—
although no mention was made of a date or time. The experience
struck her forcefully, since it seemed so much more vivid and
convincing than an ordinary dream. She was extremely upset, for
tata Bethuel was one of the most beloved members of the church.
Not knowing whom to talk to about it, she went to a church
member who in the West would be called a psychic or spiritualist
and asked him to determine if the dream was a true prophecy. He
was convinced that it was. Although she did not want tata Bethuel
to know about her dream, word spread among the congregation
and eventually someone told him. He only laughed, for he did not
care, having "died" once before and knowing his second death
could not be far off. People began to forget about it, preferring to
deny the possibility that the dream could be true. But tata Bethuel
did die in February 1969, almost two years after the woman's
dream.

The night before he died he went to see the vice-president of
the choir, Paul Nkwala, to advise him on how to keep the choir
together, what to do if there were problems. Tata Paul became
upset and annoyed. "Why are you telling me these things?" he
asked. "You're president of the choir. Are you going somewhere?
You talk like someone going traveling."

"Today I may be here, tomorrow I may be gone," tata Bethuel
replied.

Tata Paul had not heard the story of the woman's dream about
his death. The next day he understood.

Many people leave this world without saying anything because
they are either shocked or find themselves in a state of "withdraw-
al-tightness" so they simply die in complete confusion. But as for
tata Bethuel, his first experience helped him not only to face
death but also to understand what kind of happiness it was about
to bring him.

I was so devastated by his going to the next world that I cried
every day. Then one day in August that year I had a vision. I cannot
describe my state of mind, for, although the vision occurred at
night, I was neither asleep nor awake but in a kind of third state.
Tata Bethuel appeared to me in my room wearing ragged, soiled
clothing and looking miserably unhappy. I was shocked.

"Why are you this way?" I cried.

"I am this way because of you."

"Why?"

"Because you are always unhappy, and when you are unhappy, I am too. I cannot begin to enjoy my life here until you stop being unhappy."

Since there was no way for him to come back, he explained, there were only two possible ways to resolve this impasse: either I came to where he was or I would accept his death, change my outlook, and go on with my life. He gave me a date in November as a deadline for deciding one way or the other. Although he did not specify the year, I assumed it to be the current year. Nevertheless, until a few years ago I continued to pay attention each year to that date.

After that vision, I came to terms with his death and no longer felt sad. In his last letter he had said he would always be around to help me. My vision seemed to be a proof of it.

The next case deals with a refugee from Angola who was converted to my elder half-brother's religious sect in Kinshasa. The man was hospitalized for kidney failure. Since he had no relatives except his wife to visit him, my brother urged me to bring food to him every day. During this time we became close friends. Anytime I failed to show up he was terribly sad. I would sometimes arrive at 5:00 P.M. and stay with him until 7:30, the closing time for visitors. I did not mind being with him this long, for I was on vacation and, there being no summer jobs for students, I had little else to do. His illness grew worse day by day. In mid-September I left Kinshasa to go back to school in Kisangani. Shaking his hand, I knew in my heart that I would not see him again, without, however, giving him the opportunity to detect my feelings and concern.

The combination of unqualified physicians and lack of proper medicine made his survival impossible. Two or three days after my return to Kisangani, he went into a deep coma. He could neither move nor take medicine. His doctor was very pessimistic and one night suggested to his wife not to return home but rather to stay with her husband, for the doctor did not think that he would be alive the next day. Even as the doctor spoke, the man stopped breathing. Minutes later, his body was cold. Alone now, the wife began to weep until her eyes were red and swollen. She spent most of the night beside her husband, waiting devotedly for the next day when other mourners could join her.

Unexpectedly, around 1:00 in the morning, her husband returned to life. He spoke to his wife with full power as if he had never been in a coma. Unlike tata Bethuel, he did not ask his wife why she was crying. He just told her that he had been in a strange but peaceful world. He was walking very fast without knowing where he was going. Though the road was very wide, it was more difficult to walk than one would wish, because there were too many people going in the same direction. He did not talk to any of them. After walking for a long time, he found himself in front of a huge door with Jesus standing in the middle. Jesus greeted him and told him that he was expecting him that night, but unfortunately he could not let him in as his record of monthly offering to the church *(kalati kia minkayulu)* was not up to date. Jesus then ordered him to return and pay his due to the church before being admitted to this new world. It must be noted that the religious sect to which he belonged is very strict regarding offerings to the church. He was disappointed to leave the paradisal atmosphere he was already enjoying. But had he the power to argue with Jesus? Looking back, all he saw was his wife weeping. He was quite confused; while it had taken hours to get there, it did not take him a minute to return to this room at the hospital. He begged his wife to go home and get his monthly record. She was terrified, afraid of her husband who had died and now was alive again and afraid to walk in the streets of Kintambo, an old, rough section of Kinshasa, at the time everyone was in bed. Their house was in the worst area.

Despite her fears, she had no choice but to go. She was accompanied by tata Aaron Wanimbu, a *mbikudi* (literally, prophet) from the same religious sect, who lived near the hospital. They went to the house to get the offering record. After tata Wanimbu paid with his own money what the "returnee" owed the church, they went back to the hospital where the husband was eagerly awaiting his record of offerings. Tata Wanimbu handed it to him, and in a matter of minutes he was dead, to everyone's amazement.

Instead of crying, his wife and friend now prayed, thanking God for giving him the opportunity to be saved. To make the deceased happier they decided to bury him with his kalati.

The final case concerns Mrs. Montini,[4] whom I met frequently between 1967 and 1972 at my cousin Jacques' private clinic in Kinshasa Gombe. I was introduced to her by my cousin because as I was planning to attend the department of religion at the Université Libre du Congo (later the University of Zaire at Kisangani), he thought Mrs. Montini's story would greatly enhance my personal faith and career as a future servant of the church.

She was a devoted Christian even before her first death. This death came as a surprise. She became briefly sick and died. Her kin and even she herself believed that it was due to kindoki. She could not tell me precisely the time when she died. At one point she was sleeping, but she was not positive whether it was at this time that she left this world for the "unknown." There was no clear division between the end of her earthly existence and the beginning of her "beyond death" existence. All of a sudden she was en route to her final destiny without, however, being aware of it. As her existence was never interrupted, she rejected the use of the verb "to die" in our talk because, as she often put it, "How can I claim that I was dead when in reality I never was? I moved from one place [world] to the other without any interruption. It was an automatic move." On her way she saw countless numbers of people heading in the same direction. She saw hardly anyone who was resting. What she saw did not impress her, for it was the same kind of scene she had always known in her lifetime; that is why she did not think the spiritual world is in the sky, as Christianity teaches.

Walking as fast as she could, she finally arrived at a place where she was unable to move any farther. It was the end of the road. People there were holding nkanda wa moyo, the book of life. As her name was in the book, she was allowed to pass. She found herself in the middle of the most beautiful city; it was very clean. All the houses were small but beautiful. To obtain the key to her room, she was referred to a man named Abraham and then to a certain Peter, who was to give her the room.[5] She had hardly spoken to Peter when he told her that the room he was supposed to give her was already reserved for another newcomer. He then asked her how she had gotten there, since it was not yet her time. She could not tell him anything, for she did not know herself how she had gotten there, that is, she had no part in it. But Peter would not listen. He urged her to return to where she had come from. Captivated by the beauty of the city, she begged him not to send her back. But it was to no avail. When he invited her to look back, suddenly all she could see was the coffin in which she was being laid down. Surprised, she called out, "Why have you put me in this coffin? I am not dead." The mourners were astonished and speechless.

Later they told her that she had been placed in the coffin because she was dead and was about to be buried. She refused to accept that she had been dead. And since her return to this world she resents this life and is eager to go back to that beautiful city she hardly had time to know.

Such fascinating stories and revelations strengthen people's belief in their interpretation of death as a gateway to a better life for those who live in compliance with society's norms.

Reaction of Survivors

If death is an opening to another life, a continuation of the present one, why are people troubled when it strikes? For anyone unacquainted with Manianga society, an incompatibility would seem to exist between how BaManianga interpret the meaning of death in a positive sense and how, in practice, they react with mourning, especially when it takes away a good member of the community. But in their own minds, such an incompatibility does not exist.

No one easily accepts the separation of oneself from a loved person without publicly expressing one's grief. Even if the loved person goes on to a better life, he or she will still be sorely missed. A kinsman who leaves the community to join the army is mourned in the same way as if he had died. He is to be wept over, for it will take years or even decades for the community to see him again. In the event he is killed, they will never see him again.

A student who is to attend school away from home is likewise to be mourned. For example, while I was working a summer job in

1972 in Kingoyi region I helped to comfort a community that was mourning a dear member who decided to attend the National University of Zaire at Lubumbashi, about a thousand miles from Kingoyi. He had just graduated from high school and, since he was the first member of that community to finish high school, he had been expected to work and make a lot of money (then about sixty dollars a month; today the pay is even less than it was in 1972) to help the needy community. But not only did he refuse to bow to its will, he decided to attend the campus farthest away, because, as he put it, "The farther, the more devoted I will be to my studies."

For an entire week members of the community wept for him, for a number of reasons. In their view, the boy did not need more education to make good money and support them. Besides, he was going too far away; some might never see him again or get to taste the fruits of his work. But in addition to this interest in his economic responsibility, their weeping was also simply a concrete way to express their love for him. As the first high school graduate in the community, he was unique, and his uniqueness made him a very important kin. He had become the light of the community in dealing with the outside world, and now he was lost to them.

To cry, to mourn, to weep publicly, therefore does not necessarily mean to be saddened or helpless in the face of death. It may imply a variety of attitudes that can only be understood in the context of each case. Generally, there are two kinds of weeping, which may express positive feelings as well as a sense of loss: reciprocal, as when two friends or relatives who have not seen each other for years weep for joy when they meet, and one-sided weeping, when one person or group weeps while the other watches passively. For example, a dead person is wailed over not because he no longer exists but because the comfort of his physical presence is now gone. In this sense weeping can be defined as an expression of the feeling of attachment between persons or groups, as in the case of the boy who was wept over by his kanda when he decided to attend the university at Lubumbashi. Or it can express a feeling of liberation. For example, people may weep at a ndoki's death not because they loved or miss him but rather because they are overjoyed to be finally free of his nightly threats. To understand weeping at funerals, then, one must take into account all the possibilities involved. It will be seen that none of them really contradict the belief in a life beyond death.

J. Decapmaeker spent most of his time studying BaKongo funerals, but he failed to understand the true meaning of weeping. For him, when people weep for the dying it is to be understood only as an expression of the feeling of attachment:

> The black man loves his own, and if there is any day when this feeling overwhelms him to the point of total preoccupation, and in a very demonstrative way, it is surely that of death. As soon as its approach is certain for a member of his family, he is careful to inform the relatives whom he can reach, so that they may come to give comfort in the last moments with a respectful attitude, that is, with legs crossed.[6]

On the other hand, when they do not weep for the dying member, it is to be understood as an expression of their anger toward him:

> Going through a village, I have seen a young man, a well known lawbreaker, accidentally dying and abandoned by everyone; he took with him the curse of the family, who did not want to pay him the least attention.[7]

What he claims here is an exception rather than the generality. No rule requires people to avoid attending the funeral of an evil member. Rather, they are socially obligated to attend, wail for, and bury him. However, their wailing may not be an expression of sadness; some may even be weeping only because they are reminded of a dear relative who has previously died.

When death strikes a good member, people are dismayed primarily because they focus on the physical separation. They cannot now communicate except through dreams, if anyone is lucky enough to see him in that way. The death of a good individual is seen as a cause for more severe grief to those who remain than to the dead person, because death means happiness and joy. It frees the dead person from every earthly evil and all worries.

Leave-Taking

When a man with a leading role is about to die, he invites to his
bedside all his closest kin to advise them on how to adjust to his
departure. If anyone is not present, he urges the others to look for
the absent one first (assuming he still has some time left before he
goes), before he speaks out. As soon as the absent one walks in,
the dying person addresses the assembly in this way:

> I am pleased to see you all
> Before my departure to our ancestors.
> I know very well the way you feel in this moment
> But I must beg you not to be so saddened.
> You must continue to love one another.
> You must protect well our ancestors' land.
> Never sell it.
> There may be someone among you and others
> Who did not like me.
> I ask him to forgive me now.
> I have nothing against anyone.
> I loved everybody.
> I am not troubled to join my ancestors.
> Again, do not be so saddened, for we will meet again.[8]

(For the Kikongo text, see the appendix.)

Then he reveals his debts, those he is entitled to collect and
those he owes. He also reveals the place where his savings are
hidden and advises on how to use them.[9] Finally, holding the
hand of the man who is to succeed him, he blesses him:

> It is now time for me to go.
> Kanda (moyo) is here.
> Do not discriminate
> Between the older and the younger;
> They are all under your leadership.
> All the kanda segments
> Are yours.
> Kanda (moyo) is now under your leadership.
> You are to share whatever you have.

> Lead and be healthy, so that you can have enough food.
> That your sisters and brothers will eat.
> Ah tu . . . tu [that is, he spits saliva on his hands].[10]

(For the Kikongo text, see the appendix.)

The ceremony over, he enters into his final state, disinterestedness in his extinguishing life. Eagerly waiting for the last minute, he remains silent. No one will ever talk to him again. Indeed, it is sinful for an individual to disturb the dying when he is in the waiting moment; in some communities the offender may be cursed or made to pay a fine. This fine may be used to pay burial expenses. In 1969, a wife in Kinshasa was heavily criticized for not observing the rule against speaking to the dying who had withdrawn to the final state. Her husband, who was in good health and ready to go to work, suddenly was dying. He did not inform her of this. She was about to set out for the market to sell bread. The load was so heavy that she called her husband, who was sitting in the living room, to help her carry the load on his bicycle. She had no idea that he was in his final moment. As requested, he carried the bread to the market for her, but on his way back home he collapsed and fell; and that was the end of his earthly life. Not only was the wife harassed for what she had done, she was requested to return to her kanda immediately after the burial. She was forced to leave behind everything she had. It was an unjustified punishment, for she had not been aware of what was happening to her husband. But some communities have no sympathy in enforcing the traditions. On the other hand, some of these traditions are becoming a thing of the past in many families, those having well-educated members.

Funeral Rites and Mourning

The period of mourning begins as soon as the dying person stops breathing. Since death is a matter of communal concern both within the kanda and beyond its boundaries, everyone must be informed. First and foremost it is announced by the piercing, mournful cries of women who have been ministering to the dying person:

What sadness, what sadness
What has happened to you
What can I do now
(Yaya bunsana, yaya bunsana
Yaya kabwebweni e e
Yaya bwene se e e)

Sometimes death is announced by a gunshot, but this is usually done only when a very important or old person dies; otherwise the normal way of sending messages beyond the village is to beat the wooden gong, *nkonzi*. Nkonzi is fashioned from a three- or four-foot length of log, up to eighteen inches in diameter, that has been hollowed out, leaving a long narrow open slit along one side. With two thick sticks fashioned for the purpose, the gong is beaten upon the center of the opening, producing a sound that carries great distances. The gong is kept in the church when not in use, and since it is also used by Christians as a call to worship, it is necessary to make a clear distinction between the announcements of worship and death. A conventional death-rhythm was introduced: *kia-di,* sad-ness, *kia-di,* sad-ness, *kia-di,* sad-ness . . . (the rhythm is very slow), followed by *Nzambi umbokele Nzambi umbokele,* God has called him (here the rhythm becomes very fast). The boys play it as hard as possible so that all the nearby communities can hear it.

As soon as the people get the news, they begin to gather. They come from every corner of the area—well dressed, half dressed, they all come in the same clothes they were wearing when the message surprised them. While men sit dejectedly outside the house of the dead wondering what to do and how to do it, women who are the most closely related sit inside around the bier to carry out two assigned duties: weeping, and cooling the body of the deceased by fanning and wiping him with their *bitambala,* head kerchiefs. They are the ones who bear most of the responsibility of showing tearfully and grievously how much the departed member was loved during his lifetime.

Guest women are neither required by any formal rule to wail, nor prohibited. But as death strikes everywhere, the women are constrained to wail (as they look to the future) for three basic reasons. First, "giving back" or "return giving" (*tuba kitemo* or *vutula kitemo*): it is a kind of association; today we cry for you, tomorrow we will cry for me. A kanda where women are not active in attending funeral services cannot expect much help from outside in time of death. The female philosophy of weeping can be summarized thusly: "Today you are grieving and I am standing by your side to help you; tomorrow it might be my turn and I will expect you to help me, too. Let us then weep together now." Second, some weep for their own loved one or ones who died years ago, and not for the deceased who is lying on the bed. They weep for remembrance. And third, others weep by moral obligation. Any woman with "strong eyes," that is, a woman who has no tears at command, is a disgrace to her kanda, friends, and husband.

Their wailing officially inaugurates *dizi,* the funeral period. Generally speaking, there are three days of funeral: the first is a day of dismay, turmoil, social disorder, unrest, and disbelief. For the stricken family it is a day when life seems insignificant. Some threaten to take their own lives because they feel it is better to go with the dead rather than face a bleak future. There are those who do not recover from first-day shock for the rest of their lives. Henri Junod writes about the Thongas of Southern Africa:

> death is not only a sad event, a great cause of pain on account of the bereavement, but a dreadful contaminating power which puts all objects and people in the neighborhood of the deceased, all his relatives, even those dwelling far away, working in Johannesburg for instance, into a state of uncleanness. This uncleanness is very dangerous indeed. It kills, if not properly treated.[11]

This "contamination" takes the form of depressed or negative thinking, an inability to function normally, because of being caught up in another's death. This has happened to me, and it made me sensitive to its occurrence in others. The following case is a perfect example.

Nsonde Josephine was a widow about fifty years of age with three children, all living in Matadi. She was very confused, her thinking incoherent. Contrary to BaManianga's normal communalism, she disliked company; and being lonely, she had a difficult time getting by in day-to-day matters. She talked very little about her problem. I met her one Sunday in 1972 when I was conducting a "without walls" service in her village in the Kingoyi area. She was not an active Christian but took the opportunity to attend, and her knowledge that I came from the university impelled her to speak about her problem with me.

"I am delighted that you can have time to talk with me," Josephine said.

"How can I be of help to you?" I asked.

"I would be happy if you could help me leave this village. I have had enough. I need a change. Life has become unbearable in this place."

"Would you like to be specific? In other words, would you like to tell me the cause of your unhappiness?"

"I do not know."

"What do you mean? If you are not ready to tell me, then why have you invited me here?"

"I'm sorry, the only reason I claimed I do not know is that I have already discussed my problem with several other people but no one has given me the help I badly need. As a result I have become more frustrated, so that unconsciously I have withdrawn into myself, I have become a lonely woman in a communal society."

"My only interest is for you to tell me your problem. I am not interested in others' failure to help you."

"My problem began when my mother died unexpectedly. The whole of my life I had lived with her until the day of her death."

"How could you live with her the whole of your life and still be married?"

"Even when I was married I still lived with her because my husband was from this village. I went to the fields [makanga] with her."

"Now can you tell me how she died?"

"She was healthy. We went to fetch firewood, but on our way back to the village it started raining. The rain was so heavy that we could hardly see. Suddenly my mother was struck and killed by lightning. Without warning she was gone." Then Josephine spoke in a very shaky voice: "I lost consciousness and stayed there until we were discovered. I did not even cry because I had no knowledge of what had happened. As it grew dark, and after it had rained so hard, my husband began to wonder where I was. He went to my mother's house, but she was not at home either. Then with my uncle and younger brother, they started looking for us. They were calling us, and hearing their calls, I began to cry loudly. They heard me and came to where we were. It was quite a trauma." She began to cry again.

"But that was a long time ago," I said. "Are you still under that shock?"

"Certainly. It will never go away."

"Are you saying that you do not want to accept that your mother is indeed dead?"

"Not exactly."

"Then why do you not try to adjust to your new life? The way you are acting gives me the impression that you do not want your mother to enjoy her new life. You must understand that when you are happy she is happy, and when you are not she is not. Consequently, you do not want your mother to be happy."

"I want her to be very happy, and enjoy her new life. As for myself, I will only be happy when I will join her again."

"You are acting as if death were the end of everything."

"How can you claim it is not the end when it takes away my mother and my husband within a period of two years? If you were me, what would you do?"

"If I tell you what I would do, would you believe?"

"Only if it makes sense to me."

"You must know that whether you accept the reality of your loved ones' deaths or not, there will be no change. Do we not say 'Maza matiamukini ka malendi totwa diaka ko' (There is no way to retrieve water lost on the ground)?"

Silence.

"Are you getting the picture now?" I asked her.

"Yes. But I do not see how I can easily return to a happy life."

"If you have the will to try it, it will be easy. You are not the first to lose a very dear one. I lost my father too. But contrary to your life, mine is a happy one."

"You are the first one to tell me this. Now I begin to see that I have been acting like a child."

She promised to change and lead a meaningful life again. To conclude our conversation we appealed to her ancestors and her mother to liberate her from her suffering. She returned to her house with a new vision and hope. The following day I saw her going to the fields with other women.

Women are generally expected to pay a higher price in be- reavement behavior than are men, who usually remain in mourn- ing for a briefer period. The weight of this expectation may have contributed to Nsonde Josephine's "contamination" by the death of her mother.

The first day of the funeral sets the tone for the entire mourning period. The level of agony is dictated by the reputation of the deceased. A good member's death produces an open crisis within the kanda. In many ways, the deceased remains irreplaceable. A famed nganga, university graduate, hunter, farmer, nzonzi (judge), chief—all these people are unique and to have one like them again may take years or even generations. When the kanda is in desperate need of something but does not know which way to turn, everyone begins to think of the deceased member who otherwise would know what to do or how to handle pressure from the outside.

The Kingoyi kanda in Banza-Lele village, district of Kivunda, has yet to overcome the loss of its famed chief, Mbelolo. According to what his kanda says, he was a chief whose prime concerns were to protect each member from ndoki's attacks or threats (during his rule there was no death believed to have been caused by ndoki) and to provide enough food for everyone. To succeed in this role he worked very hard. Before relying on others, he relied first upon himself.

As a result of Mbelolo's example, each chief is evaluated accord- ing to how close he comes to Mbelolo's merits. His death has had an irretrievable consequence: the kanda thinks of him because his death lessened the political, religious, and economic power it enjoyed during his lifetime. As it has not yet replaced him, it is still symbolically participating in his death from time to time. As long as the gap produced by his death is not closed, social disturbance will be chronic in that kanda; it will always be in search of a new identity. As Benjamin C. Ray writes,

> At first, new problems of social and spiritual identity arise. When a
> family loses one of its members, especially a senior member, a

significant moral and social gap occurs. The family together with other kinsmen must close this gap and reconstitute itself through a series of ritual and social adjustments. . . .[12]

And A. R. Radcliffe-Brown adds:

For the society a death is the loss of one of its members, one of its constituent parts. A person occupies a definite position in society, has a certain share in the social life, is one of the supports of the network of social relations. His death constitutes a partial destruction of the social cohesion, the normal social life is disorganized, the social equilibrium is disturbed. After the death the society has to organize itself anew and reach a new condition of equilibrium.[13]

In this respect, death causes a partial destruction of the communal life, and this destruction sometimes remains irremediable. As for the deceased himself, though he has ceased to be a member of the living kanda, his influence has not stopped. It rather becomes greater than before.

Usually people are at ease with the death of an old man or woman, more so than with the death of a young person. They are happy to see old persons go, for they do not expect much from them. They have successfully completed the cycle of earthly existence—childhood, youth, adulthood, and obsolescence or "return to childhood"—and now deserve a complete rest. Jack Goody expresses a similar view about the LoDagaba, the LoSaala, and the LoWili:

It can therefore be understood that in all these communities the older the deceased, the more joking at his funeral; for the loss is less acutely felt than in the case of a younger man. A fundamental difference exists between the attitude to death of a person who has lived his full span and produced male heirs, and to that of a younger man dead before his time. The first allows of a gradual alienation from the network of jural and individual ties; the community anticipates the readjustment required. On the other hand, an unexpected death causes a sudden rent in the fabric of relationships and makes greater demands upon the system.[14]

While the impact of an expected death is small, that of an unexpected one is great; it is more expensive both economically and socially, for no one has been preparing for it. It is a hard blow to accept and absorb. Therefore, when the news of an unexpected death breaks, the initial reaction of the affected kin is a kind of craziness. At this moment everyone openly manifests bitterness about being alive. The general mood of the moment is that it is better to go with the dead person. People want to take their own lives, but on the other hand they are eager to preserve them. (I have never seen a case of an individual's actually committing suicide to protest the death of a loved one.)

As seen in the three case studies of return from death, it takes time for the deceased to reach his final destination. The general feeling among most of my informants is that the deceased does not leave the mourning house before burial. He stays in the same house, checking how his departure is being handled and also waiting for the ancestors to formally open the door for him to join their community. Before the burial takes place, then, he is in a state of "between-ness" or "communityless-ness." Physically he is no longer part of the community because he is dead and has gone to the other world; spiritually, however, he is still alive in the living community, and because of this belief they still talk to him until the last minute, the time of burial. Then they offer him their last gifts, as Wyatt MacGaffey describes:

> Beginning the morning after a death occurs, the elders sit under a convenient mango tree, listening to the presentation of speeches of those who bring *lusadusu* (help, from *sadisa*) to the clan of the deceased. This procedure is called the *mafundu*. At one time contributions took the form of blankets in which the body was wrapped. Speakers now refer more or less elaborately to their gifts in terms of the blankets and other cloths for which money is now substituted. Children and *bankwezi* are expected to contribute the "blankets that go underneath"; the Father offers "blankets to go on top." Various other denominations are possible. In addition to cash gifts, actual blankets, sheets, and bedspreads are given, particularly by closer relatives. Many of these bedclothes are in fact wrapped around the body; others go into storage as part of the funeral fund of the lineage. People who give blankets usually give cash as well. . . .[15]

Spiritually, the dead remains part of the old living community as well as the new community of the ancestors, until all the rites of adjustment to his departure are properly observed and completed. In the meantime, he remains a public charge to those closely related to him, a public charge in the sense that they adjust their way of life according to his present status, namely, "betweenness." While on one hand he belongs to both communities, the living and the dead, on the other hand he belongs to neither. He is a member without identity.

Sometimes the community elects to mourn its departed member outside the house in an enclosure of palm leaves built by bana bambuta (children on the father's side of the family). As MacGaffey writes,

> As soon as possible a rectangular enclosure *(lupangu)* of palm leaves is put up outside the house of the deceased or in some other convenient place. It must be large enough to accommodate all those who attend the overnight wake. In the center is a flat-roofed, unenclosed shelter where the body reposes, usually on the deceased's own bed. It is wrapped in sheets and blankets with the face showing, or just the eyes and the forehead, and is covered with embroidered bedspreads or the like. When Lufumba's body was brought out the women present were actively curious, some of them scrambling for the best places close to the bier. As soon as the body was in place one of the children led the group in a little ceremony frequently repeated throughout the mortuary rites: everybody, kneeling, raises his forefinger to the sky, then points it downward, then claps his hands; the handclap is repeated, on command, five times, this number being mentioned aloud. . . . In the four sides of the *lupangu* there are, or should be, four doors belonging to *nkazi, se,* and the two *mfumu za n'teekudi,* each of whom closes his door when he arrives by hanging up a blanket or bedspread in the opening. After a door has been closed people who wish to go through are supposed to make an obeisance *(sakila),* though few do. An extra entrance provided for informal going in and out does not count as one of the doors. The body in the shelter is respectfully referred to as "Kongo."[16]

This custom is popular among Christians who belong to African independent churches. These churches, which have separated from missionary churches, have incorporated elements of traditional belief and because of this are usually considered syncretic.

In his description, MacGaffey observes that the members performing the rite inside the enclosure kneel down, raise their hands to the sky, point them downward, then clap their hands (and also their feet) at least five times. MacGaffey did not understand the meaning of this rite. I happened to belong (from 1960 to 1963) to a sect which performs this rite at the death of a member. The religious belief is that at precisely this time the two worlds come together. The number five refers to (1) God (the Christian God, who is not quite the same as their forefathers' God);[17] (2) Nzambi, the traditional God; (3) Jesus, son of the Christian God; (4) ancestors, Nzambi's servants and guardians of the living community; and (5) the living community, those who belong to their movement. These five all meet together when there is a death. The people prefer to perform the rite in an open enclosure rather than in a closed house because unlike the Christian God, who is usually thought of as being locked up in the church, the traditional God cannot be limited to one place, for he is everywhere. This belief is stronger among the young educated members.

The end of the first day, that is, the eve of the second day, is marked by persistent wailings by old women and those who have just arrived. But contrary to the disorderly wailing during the day, night wailing is well coordinated because both women and men are to participate for the first time. Though men do not wail, they are to sing mournful songs through the night. And very often they set the tone of the night, for if they are persistent singers, women are likely to join them. To distract the women from wailing, the men sing the most popular songs, such as:

> We strangers, we travelers
> Are passing by this world
> And are going to reunite
> With our family in our country.

> Our new country in our new world
> In the Lord's complete world
> Neither is there suffering nor wailing
> Only joy in that country (world).

> Jesus Christ preceded
> To build houses which we will occupy
> To make feast to his own
> And glorify them.

All who have succeeded
Are now resting
And are only waiting for us
In eternal joy.

Because of that joy
We will forget all our sufferings now
What we failed to do we will do
What is hidden we will see.

In clean clothes, eternal honor,
New names, everything new
We will see everything including
God our father and will be like him.[18]

And also:

O father, I am supported by
Your power, my father.
Glory to my Lord my God
Alleluia our Lord.

Let us sing glory
Alleluia the king of heaven
Who is powerful and will reign forever
He is my Lord my God.

(For the Kikongo texts, see the appendix.)

They sing these songs in an ordered and serious manner. Designated boys play drums and *ngongi,* a kind of small metallic bell struck with a stick. In such excitement as this, nobody dares to slumber; to do so would be repellent to the rest of the community. The whole night the people remain in this atmosphere, but at midnight for about thirty minutes the focus shifts to the deceased himself. A spokesman designated by the family members of the dead person calls upon the deceased to be brave and ready to begin his long journey to join the *bakulu,* ancestors. The spokesman exhorts him not to be afraid, for he has brothers, sisters, mothers, fathers, cousins, children, aunts, and uncles out there who are ready to assist him and make the transition easier.

In the meantime, bana bambuta (children on the father's side) are busy the whole night; they are to see that everyone has tea or coffee at any time. It is important to note that before the burial no alcohol is to be served. This is to avoid drunkenness, the root of disorder and trouble.

After the all-night singing, the second day starts on a lower note. It is the most relaxed of the three days. Nobody wails but the latecomers. Those who are not closely associated with the stricken kanda may sometimes take a break and briefly go home to take care of any business they left unfinished upon hearing of the death. However, they are to limit their activities to the vicinity of the house; whoever returns to his fields to continue his work while the deceased is not yet buried is harshly judged and becomes a disgrace to his family, for he has not respected his fellow human being. But nobody really would do such a thing.

For the family of the deceased, however, there is not much difference between this day and the first day. Though they do not cry loudly, they are still crying within their hearts and most still refuse either to eat or drink because, as they say, "It makes no sense to eat or drink at the time your departed loved one is perhaps experiencing the most difficult time in his life." They are more concerned with his life than with their own. This is the main reason that the mourning period may take months or even years among immediate family members.

The preparations for the burial start on this day. People begin to bring their contributions: money, sheets, blankets, and other gifts. Nothing is refused. With the money, the family buys food for the public and pays the carpenter who is to build the coffin. The remaining money (if any) can be given to the deceased's children to buy clothing or food. A well-attended funeral means more money, sheets, and blankets. In this case, those affected by the death are saved from borrowing money to meet the expenses.

Attendance at a funeral has several motivations. First, it may be a personal aim: an individual who is active in attending funerals in his area is assured that the day he dies, his funeral will also be well attended. Regardless of his personal behavior, people will be constrained to attend because of what he has done for them at the time they needed almost everyone's participation. Attending his funeral is the way of thanking him for what he has done in the past. Accordingly, he who does not bother to attend funerals can be sure that his own death will attract only a few people.

Second, there is kanda pride. A kanda deeply involved in the community's affairs is well respected. And this can only be possible if its members are active in attending communal events such as funerals, marriages, and births. Their attendance can then be regarded as an investment for themselves and their kanda. Sometimes the death of an individual who does not usually attend others' deaths may attract a large number of people to pay their respects not to the deceased but to the kanda, if it is a well-respected one. And this respect overshadows its member's isolation.

Third, fear of the dead also encourages attendance at a funeral. As personal involvement is considered a kanda investment, and since the dead are still members of the kanda, any individual who does not contribute to the well-being of the kanda may be reprimanded and even punished by his ancestors. Their fear, then, is a motivation for the living to attend, so that they may not jeopardize their investment in the welfare of the whole kanda now and in the future.

And finally, there is simply personal gratification. Hungry people are active in attending public events not because they want to make an investment for their makanda but because they are hungry and know that there is plenty of food at a community gathering. They attend to satisfy hunger rather than to pay their respects to the deceased and to his *kanda*. Because of their poverty, they make no contribution at all; they become public charges, but no one can deny them the opportunity to attend. To do so would be a violation of social rules and expectations. Thus they are always welcome.

The third day of the funeral generally starts in a depressed mood. Everyone knows that this is the last day to be physically associated with the dead person. Kinfolk—widow or widower, children, sisters, brothers, father and mother (if still living), uncles, and sometimes close friends—are the most affected. It is during this day that they begin to feel the pain of loss. Involved parties now fall into one of two categories: those who have gone from grief to resignation and acceptance, to an adjustment to the loss; and those who are still grieving. They have gone from grief to resignation and then to grief again, followed by withdrawal into *mvindu,* a massive retreat into a negligence even of basic hygiene and therefore dirtiness.

For children and their mother (if the deceased was a husband and father), it means that the time has come to pack their belongings and return to the mother's village. It is the most agonizing day because not only are they to bury their father, they are to leave their house, fields, and friends. They begin to experience the pain of isolation. It would not be misleading to say that the unity or togetherness of the first two days no longer holds.

Without doubt the most affected of all are the helpless children, when the parental kanda requires their exit from their father's house and their return to their mother's village or clan-section. The following case illustrates what it means to be deprived of one's father in Manianga society.

This story concerns my cousins. During their father's lifetime they had a happy life. He did his best to ensure that his children had a good life, lacking nothing. They did not know how to be greedy or eager for anything. Their father was the most famed hunter in the entire region. And because of his exceptional skills, they enjoyed a high standard of living (as far as standards of living in the countryside are concerned). Most of the time they ate meat, even though there are people who do not eat meat the entire year because they cannot afford it. The plan of his house came from Kinshasa and the house had been built by the most respected masons of the area. Swedish missionaries from the Sundi-Lutete Mission who went to preach in his village stayed overnight in his house. And though he lacked any formal education himself, he had plans to send his children to school in France and Belgium. That plan was not realized, because he died before they were old enough.

Because of his material success, his children completely ignored their maternal kanda. Their father made no attempt to encourage them to visit from time to time their maternal uncles, the ones who would take care of them in the event of his death. Fully aware of what might lie ahead, their mother privately urged them to be closer to their maternal uncles than to their father, since the society is matrilinear by descent. Not only did they refuse her advice, they mocked her, claiming that they could not be associated with their uncles for fear that their uncles might eat them through their kindoki. Besides, they did not believe that their healthy father could die before they grew up.

They took for granted that their father's kanda was their kanda.
The day their father unexpectedly died, they understood how
wrong their assumptions had been. After the burial of their father,
their paternal uncle, who was next in line to become the head of
the kanda, firmly requested that they leave the house so that he
could move into it. As night had already fallen, he allowed them to
wait until the next day before returning to their mother's village.
They were so upset and confused that they cried the whole night.
Instead of one loss, they had to deal with two irreplaceable losses.
At one point, the other paternal uncles suggested to the leader
that he allow them to stay until the end of the mourning period,
which would take several months; but eager to enjoy the
luxurious life his brother had left behind, he refused to compromise. He kept everything for himself but their clothes and
what their mother had bought with her own money. Money their
father had saved for emergencies was taken by their uncle, the
new leader. Not only did he take everything from them, he
ridiculed and laughed at their unexpected misery.

Early in the morning they took what they were allowed and
headed for their mother's village. Because of their past in-
difference, their maternal kanda gave them a chilly reception.
They had no house of their own, and no one bothered to give
them one. Although Manianga society is traditionally com-
munalist, there was in this case no spirit of communalism. They
faced the most difficult time of their lives. Before they could build
their own house, their mother's brother, who could not totally
reject them, allowed them to sleep in his small house. Their
mother chose to live in an abandoned kitchen about three hundred meters from the rest of the family. In her isolation she was
visited one day by *mbamba,* one of the deadliest snakes in the
region. She was too afraid even to think of running away. Fortunately the snake did not harm her.

Not knowing how to survive in this hostile milieu, the two
first-born sons secretly visited their father's grave, and this is how
they addressed him, according to my cousin Paul, the eldest son
of the family:

> Father, do not be surprised about our secret
> Visit. Since you left us
> There is no word to describe our suffering.

We believe that you are aware of our new life.
The day we accompanied you here
Was the day we were requested to leave
The house. Father Makonko is now the owner
Of your house. According to him this is his
Time to speak out, ours has passed.
Everything you left for us, even our own
Money we were saving,
Became his. We took nothing with us when we
Went to mother's village. And due to our
Arrogance toward mother's kanda
The day we got there there was no one to care
For us. We have become laughingstocks.
Some dare to call us stupid boys.
As for paternal aunts,
They would prefer us to stay in your house
But paternal uncles would not listen;
They strongly urged us to leave.
We are always crying because of
Too much loneliness since you left.
Lonely mother living out of the community
Was about to be bitten by a mbamba . . .

(For the Kikongo text, see the appendix.)

Then they began to cry in front of their father's grave and left without speaking again. Returning to the village, they kept quiet and avoided informing even their own mother and brothers about their secret visit to their father's grave.

Then one night while they were sleeping, the father appeared in a dream to cousin Paul, his eldest son. He told them that he had been aware of their difficulties long before their visit. But since he could not return to look after them, the only possibility for them to survive was to work hard. He then suggested that cousin Paul, who was then fourteen years old, quit school and *baka kisalu kia mundele,* be employed by a white man. According to cousin Paul, this is what his father said:

> As I cannot return, you must leave school and look for employ-
> ment with a white man. To advance quickly it is necessary to
> become a storeman. Being a child, you will suffer at the begin-

ning. But do not be afraid, for I will be with you all the time. I will not abandon you. You are now the leader of [my] household. I am convinced that your brothers and sisters will be able to finish their studies because of you.

(For the Kikongo text, see the appendix.)

To encourage him to work, the father visited him frequently in his dreams. In October 1954 Paul left the village to hunt for work in the Mbanza-Ngungu (formerly Thysville) area. He decided to go a long distance away in order to avoid endless begging by relatives and friends, to be able to save his money and use it according to his father's wishes and instructions. It was not long before he got a job in Gombe Matadi, about fifty kilometers from Mbanza-Ngungu and two hundred kilometers from Kinshasa. Being semi-literate, he was hired as a *boy magasin,* a store helper, by a Portuguese named Fersila. Since Fersila had several stores in the Mbanza-Ngungu area, my cousin had a good opportunity to become a chief storeman.

However, before he could think the unthinkable, of being in charge of a store, he had to work as a boy. With his small salary he helped his brothers and sisters stay in school. He regularly sent them clothes and cash. In 1956 he was appointed storeman in Luidi (about 150 kilometers from Gombe Matadi). In a short time he became wealthy. There is no one in the entire kanda who did not enjoy the fruits of his success, even though the children were not well received after their father's death. He has become the most respected person not only in his own kanda but in the entire area, because he is the wealthiest individual in our particular region. The only reason he is so successful is that he has had the full benediction and support of his father. If he had not listened to that advice, he would be only an average member. This is another indication of the involvement by the dead in the affairs of the living. However, the father, it was believed, did not forgive the man who had driven away his wife and children and taken all their belongings, but cursed him. For the man became confused, was not able to lead the family, and left the village for Kasangulu, near Kinshasa. All of the fruit trees the father had planted—mango, orange, mandarin—withered and died within a few years. It seemed the father had the last laugh after all.

Finally the day comes for preparing the burial, digging the grave, and giving farewell presents to the dead member. Early in the morning, about five o'clock, bana bambuta go to Makulu, the resting place of the dead, to dig the grave. Its length and width are determined by the size of the deceased, though the average size is about four meters in length and about eighty centimeters in width. Due to the lack of efficient tools, it takes about three hours to do the job; but this also depends upon the condition of the soil. In the rainy season when the soil is soft it takes less time.

In the meantime, back in the village people are busy making their contributions, because as soon as the diggers return it will be time to clothe the corpse. It is important to present their gifts well before this. MacGaffey gives an extended and interesting description of these gifts:

> All gifts are recorded by a competent child who is chosen by the house to keep the accounts for the affair. He may be courteously addressed as Mayala, "the one in charge" (*yaala*, "to govern"). . . .
>
> Gifts are recorded under the name of the donor's clan, not on the basis of his relationship to the affair. Etiquette calls for the *nzaki* of the clan section, or at least of the house, to present the contributions of "those who stand behind him," but nowadays many individuals like to present their own so as to draw more attention to their own name. At Lufumba's funeral some 220 individual contributions were recorded, ranging from 5 to 1,000 francs. The actual number of contributions, many of them from persons related only distantly, nominally, or not at all, was larger than that. The total receipts, at an ordinary funeral, may run to about 18,000 francs; at an important funeral as much as 45,000 francs, which in the village economy is a prodigious amount of money, may be contributed. . . .[19]

Regardless of social status, all give what they can, because it is the last opportunity to show their love toward the deceased and his kanda. They also prepare the burial with great seriousness, for if the deceased is convinced that he has not been properly buried, he may return to harm his relatives. Because of this fear even unwanted members are sometimes buried with full honor to avoid their returning. As for a member who dies a thousand miles away from the community and whose body cannot be returned, a "proxy" or per absentia burial is organized to make up for what his adopted community might not do for him. It is traditionally believed that this per absentia burial is also an invitation for him to return home and live among his own relatives, both the dead and the living. Most old people who die in Kinshasa elect to be returned to their village in order to be buried at their own Makulu. Young people do not care. But even some intellectuals living in Kinshasa or abroad may request that their body be returned to their village. For example, a good friend of mine who was living in North Carolina was struck by a deadly disease. Knowing that he had no chance for survival, he decided to return to Zaire and die there rather than in America, where his spirit would not be among his own.

When everyone has given his *fundu* (gift), bana bambuta of the same sex as the deceased wash his body before putting it into the coffin. It is strictly forbidden for a member of the kanda to see the deceased's *nsoni,* penis or vagina.[20] After this last bath, bana bambuta attire the body in the best clothes they possess. To make him more comfortable, they place blankets and sheets underneath so he will not feel the pain of being in a wooden coffin. For those who cannot make the trip to Makulu, it is time to say goodbye or sometimes to emphasize their innocence if his death is believed to have been caused by kindoki. Decapmaeker writes:

> Standing before the corpse, he presents at the height of his chest his two hands open and juxtaposed, then spits a little saliva on his palms. At the same time he protests to the deceased that he is innocent of his death, and asks him to be happy to stay where he is, not to come to communicate with the living either in dreams or evil spells. [I am not sure whether Decapmaeker understood this correctly, because among the BaKongo the dead reveal their will to the living by dreams. I have yet to hear of anyone ordering any deceased except *ndoki* not to contact him through a dream. Dreams from the dead are welcome and even solicited.] If someone recalls having addressed harsh words, insults or curses to him during his lifetime, without having had time to be reconciled, he will be careful to gather a magical herb, kimbanzia, and then will come to chew it and make ritual spittings [of the juice], saying to the departed: "What I said, I said only from the surface of my tongue."[21]

At this time no one is allowed to weep; even the widow is to remain silent because if there is weeping it is believed that the deceased will be saddened rather than happy to go. Only those who cannot accompany the deceased to Makulu are allowed to speak now, and since few persons stay behind, there are very few speeches in the village. Most of the speeches are to be made at Makulu.

Generally, the burial does not take place before 4:00 P.M. The reason for this is that the mourners fear to bring the deceased to Makalu during the day at a time when spirits are believed to be busy and may not yet be home. This tradition is observed only in the villages, not in the cities.

When the time to go has arrived, two to four strong men, lined up one by one, carry the bier. The crowd follows behind in the most joyful atmosphere. They sing, play drums, even dance. They do this to make the traveler very happy. From now on weeping is a thing of the past; even the widow knows that it is not worthwhile to weep again, for nothing can be changed. But the end of the wailing does not mean a return to normal life directly after the burial.

At Makulu the actual burial is preceded by a long (and sometimes tiring) series of farewell speeches addressed to the deceased.[22] Most of the kinfolk speak, though there is no obligation to do so. All these speeches say the same thing, focusing on the good relations the speakers had with the deceased. Wishing him well in his new life and world, they sometimes urge him to harm his killer, if his death is believed not to have been caused by God:

> I do not have much to tell you,
> Just to wish you a happy travel to our ancestors (and other
>   departed ones).
> As we are about to separate, my heart is heavily
> Saddened. I am very sad
> But what else can I do? Spilled water on the ground is spilled.
> I do not know whether I will succeed in explaining to the children
>   that they
> Will not see you again.
> Do not forget us in your new world. As we are thinking of you
> Please do the same for us. It is my hope that we shall meet again.
> If your death came from God we accept it,
> But if it came from an evil human being do not let
> His soul be at peace.
> Go in peace.

(For the Kikongo text, see the appendix.) Van Wing writes that the people of the Lower Congo "ask their deceased ancestors for positive favors like a good hunt, a good harvest, fertility, etc. They go out to the graveyard, pour libations on the graves and address to their ancestral spirits prayers such as this: 'Oh, Father, oh! Elders, come to drink the salutary wine, increase fertility and human wealth.' "[23]

There are three main reasons why people speak to the deceased. First, before the final burial, the deceased is still a member of the living community. Accordingly, the people can have direct talks with him. And being still a member of the community, he is not to be addressed in the same manner or with the same respect that is directed to the other deceased members, the ancestors.

Second, since the departed one is heading toward the community of the spirits, the people take this opportunity to commission him or her as their spokesperson to those who are already there. He or she is to plead with them so that the living brothers and sisters can have a better life; this cannot be brought about without ancestors' material and spiritual support.

And third, while the good member is invited to visit the living community from time to time, the evil member, ndoki, is forcibly urged not to return and, to make sure that he or she understands what they mean, some families plant pineapple trees all over the grave. It is an invitation for the deceased to get lost forever and ever.

Throughout the ceremony, the mourners speak to the deceased in the second person because he is still one of the group. He is thought to be carefully listening to everything they tell him. This belief is confirmed when the deceased responds through dreams at night to their inquiries. Those who cannot speak to the deceased at this time may choose just to put a symbolic amount of earth on top of his bier before he is completely covered with earth.

After completing the burial, the mourners return to the village to start the next mournful period, the after-death mourning, or *mpidi.* As they arrive, they wash their hands before being reunited with those who did not make the trip. The washing of hands is a symbol of purification. Being momentarily in the kingdom of the dead, they must purify themselves before returning to their normal community.

Upon returning from Makulu, the leaders of the stricken kanda meet to decide how long this after-death mourning will be observed. The longer the period, the less intense its observance becomes. The importance of observing post-death rites is threefold: to clean the pollution and unhappiness brought by death, to suffer with the deceased in his struggle to adjust to his new life and world, and to heal the wounds caused by this death in case ndoki is suspected.

There are different kinds of rites for this period. The concerned kanda may choose to observe all or just one or two. The most frequent ones are *bendo* and *kifwidi.*

Bendo starts directly after the burial. Those most immediately affected by the death are requested to spend at least a week of inactivity to relax and recover from the three days' trauma. Guests are under no social obligation to observe this rite. However, some (mostly women) elect to stay for two or three days to help with cooking, drawing water out of the river, and fetching firewood used to cook food and to be burnt at night when people gather to chat or to discuss important matters.

During this recuperative period, it is believed, the deceased does the same thing. In the process of recovering from the shock of a perhaps unexpected departure, he makes himself known to everyone in his new after-death community; it is also the period when he learns the hows, whys, wheres, and whens of the way things work in the new community. It is mostly an exploratory period for him. His complete assimilation into the new community usually takes months or perhaps years. He is believed to be learning and growing until he reaches the rank of ancestors. Some spirits may never reach this rank if they do not have the desire. They must desire to learn so they can grow and become powerful.

During this period of adjustment, the living community observes the rite of kifwidi. Kifwidi is a rite of seclusion or retreat into *mvindu,* or personal uncleanness. The mourners believe that it is inappropriate to enjoy themselves, that is, to return to their normal way of life at the time their loved one is perhaps still experiencing the greatest difficulties of adjustment to his new life. Hence, by denying being themselves they symbolically die with him. That is, they momentarily put aside their humanness and culture. In addition, all sexual activities are to be suspended. What Jean Buxton writes about Mandari is also true among Ba-Manianga:

> Being a mourner also involves abstinence from sexual inter-course. Since the object of intercourse is seen to be to beget a child a woman must not conceive while wearing the "clothing of death" since violation of this rule offends against the Mandari dialectic of the separation of incompatibles. The action of procrea-tion belongs to life and must not be introduced into situations associated with death. To mix the two is death-dealing.[24]

To enjoy sex during this time means lack of respect for both communities, visible and invisible. The guilty member could become an outcast. (Once, whoever was caught in the act of enjoying sex might face the death penalty.)

The one who carries the heaviest burden of kifwidi is without doubt the widow. In some areas she is required to remain dirty for six to twelve months without taking a bath or washing her clothes. But since there is now much moving back and forth between the villages and the large cities and the world is becom-ing a more compact and interrelated place, this rule is beginning to be relaxed. But traditionally, if a widow acted against social expectations it would open the door to speculation that she was the ndoki who had eaten her husband. Sometimes her beautiful black hair becomes brown and ugly with dirtiness. Throughout the period she is forbidden to pass through the village; she is always to go around. She is not permitted to talk aloud; she is rather to whisper. Nor should she look straight into other peo-ple's eyes. Otherwise she will be heavily fined by her late hus-band's brothers and uncles.

Sometimes the quickest way for a widow to end her kifwidi is to be married to one of her husband's kinsmen. If she refuses such a marriage as a matter of respect to her late husband, that is, refuses to return to a good life as if nothing had happened, her husband's kanda will not hold her in contempt, because she is not required to remarry. After her husband's death she has no more obligation to his family. But occasionally she will be asked to be married by one of her husband's relatives if her husband died young after they were together only a few years; in this instance, if she refuses, a fine could be imposed on her. If her kanda cannot afford to pay such a fine (in effect, a return of the dowry), the only alternative available to her is to give herself to her kanda-in-law as *nnanga,* slave.

To make her slave status official, she brings together her brothers- and sisters-in-law. Then, taking *ngazi* (palm nut) and clippings of her own fingernails and hair, she gives them to the kanda leader to initiate her enslavement. From now on she becomes the "property" of her late husband's kanda. Her duty is to obey and perform whatever she is required to. She is not permitted to visit her kanda or have talks with her closest relatives such as brothers, sisters, or parents, if still alive. (This practice is rapidly dying out and is seldom seen today.) The widow's dead husband, who is the main cause of her enslavement, is likely to threaten his living kanda to let her return to her kanda without any requirement. But if he remains silent, she will have a difficult time if she does not find money with which to buy her freedom.

If in the meantime her kanda becomes economically sound enough to seek her liberation, the first step is no longer the repayment of the dowry. Her kanda members must first pay a symbolic (and sometimes heavy) fine for wasting too much time before settling their sister's problem. Only after both fine and dowry have been received will she become a free woman. Despite her freedom, if she is still under the restrictions of kifwidi, she will have to observe them, but they will be lessened to allow her to work and take care of herself. At this time she is entitled to wash her clothes and take a bath whenever she wishes.

When the date set for cleansing arrives, she returns to her husband's kanda to be cleansed together with all those who have observed this rite. It is a big day for everyone who participates in this rite because it is the day they are to be freed and born again; that is, when they will again become full productive members of the society. They wear their best clothes, which have been reserved for this occasion. They eat, drink, and dance the whole day and night. They enjoy themselves because they were dead and are now alive again.

As for a widower, his kifwidi is very light and does not require him to remain dirty. The only restriction he is to observe is not to get married or engage in sex. If he secretly does and is caught, he is heavily fined by his brothers- and sisters-in-law, and they ridicule him for not being able to observe the least restriction. The main reason the society avoids confining the widower with the burden of kifwidi is that he must be constantly on the move taking care of community matters, especially if he is the leader or nganga of the family.

In the case of a child's death, kifwidi is not observed. This is in order to allow him to return, to be born again to his own parents. Here Buxton's statement is helpful:

> The death of a baby affects only its parents. A still-born infant or one which dies at birth is laid in a termite mound and only the mother laments. She must then hide her grief, for "if too much notice is taken of the death of a new-born baby Creator will be angered and not send the woman another child. Creator can send one, and does not like to hear people making a fuss." The parents observe mourning for three days and then the mother is washed in hot water, the skin which she was wearing when the infant died is placed on the hut roof, and she dons a new one: when she feels fit she sleeps with her husband. An infant's social range is so limited that only parents can be adversely affected by its death.[25]

When the first child of the family dies in his early days, they bury him beside the house or by the side of the road. This is done to speed up his return. If a newborn baby is of the same sex as the first child who died, the parents are likely to give him or her the same name, on the assumption that the previous child has returned.

For example, in 1970 a couple from Mongo Luala living in Kinshasa-Bandalungwa lost their one-year-old child, Simon. He was not their first child, but he was special because their earlier and only surviving children had been born so many years before, in 1950 and 1953. Between 1953 and 1969, when Simon was born, they did have other children, but none had survived. (The parents attributed this to kindoki.) So when Simon was born, it was a big day for them. To avoid repeating the dire experience of the past, they took every imaginable precaution to guarantee his survival. They were devoted Christians, but because of what they had already witnessed they took their new baby to a ngang'a nkisi. He was asked to bless and protect the new baby with his nkisi (good spirit-power) so that bandoki would not dare to catch and eat him. The parents sought nganga's help and not the help of the Christian God because, in their own words, "the Christian God is too slow to act." They accused the Christian God of failing to protect their dead children from bandoki's attacks. They believed the only way Simon could survive was to be protected by their ancestors through nganga.

But even nganga failed to protect their baby, and he died unexpectedly. His parents were almost certain that he would come back, be born to them again. To speed up his return, he should have been buried in an isolated place such as behind the house or at the side of a road, but since they were in Kinshasa where this custom is not tolerated, they could not do it. In a last effort of hope, they wrote the following words on a piece of paper and put it in the coffin: "Your parents are expecting your immediate return." A year later, in 1971, another boy was born. He looked exactly like Simon. In their minds, there was no doubt that this was the same Simon who had come back. As expected, they named him Simon. When I last saw him before leaving Banda-lungwa for Israel in 1973, he was a healthy boy.

If a couple gives birth to twins and one of them dies, no kifwidi is observed. Otherwise the remaining twin would be sad and would follow the dead one. They are believed to be so interconnected that no one dares to upset them.

During the kifwidi rite, the leader of the group sets up a date to open the deceased's house; it is also on this date that members of the group decide whether to destroy the house or to give it to another kinsman. All the deceased's belongings are to be distributed among his kinfolk: brothers, sisters, children,[26] uncles, cousins, aunts, spouse, and sometimes close friends. No outsider is entitled to take part in the distribution because, as they say, "Inherited property is not for outsiders" (Fwa ka divwangwa kwa batantu ko). Anyone who is unrelated to the group by blood or treaty is an outsider. Each kinsman, elder or child, must receive something, no matter how small or meaningless it may be. The idea is not to become wealthy but rather to make everyone proud of his dead kinsman and the communality or togetherness continuing to bind the kanda even in time of sorrow. Knowing that his property is being used by everyone in the kanda, the deceased is certainly the most delighted of all, because those who use his property will never forget him. They will relate to him in terms of what he has left rather than what he had been during his lifetime. Consequently, a not too harmful ndoki whose property is shared and accepted by everyone in the kanda may from time to time be appreciated. For harmful ndoki, however, no kinsman will want their belongings for they are seen as evil.

Unsuccessful members who cannot manage to get by on their own labor are the ones who eagerly await the death of a prosperous member in order to inherit a share of his property. When his death occurs, there are those who weep for joy; they are happy to see him go because they are thinking about what they will receive when his belongings are distributed.

The kanda also has the right not to distribute a dead member's property. In such a case, the leader is likely to designate a trustworthy individual to be in full control of the property. He is allowed to use it, but at the time of important events such as marriages or deaths, he is to place it at everyone's disposal. If he has misused it, he may be fined or requested to replace it.

After kifwidi, another mourning rite, matanga, may take place. This rite may occur only once or twice in one's lifetime. It is aimed at honoring all the members who died since the last matanga. It is not very popular for economic reasons: it requires a lot of money and energy. All the tombs of those dead members who are to be honored must now be built in bricks and cement. After this has been done, a date is set for the biggest party of one's lifetime. People come from every corner of the region, bringing gifts of money, goats, sheep, wine, *mpata* (the most expensive traditional food), and other things. To make up the cost of the feast, the organizers build an enclosure in which they sell the best food and drink at a high price. Those who cannot afford to eat inside can still eat outside without charge. However, personal and community pride being at stake, everyone tries to save as much as possible ahead of time in order to eat in the enclosure. Since this uncommon feast attracts hundreds of people, the profit of the organizers is significant. With this money they pay their debts and share the rest among themselves, that is, the members of the whole kanda. The length of matanga may vary from community to community. In some areas it may take a whole week. All members living in cities are expected to attend this important event. Those who cannot attend for reasons beyond their control, such as poor health or obligation to a job, happily send any amount of cash they can afford.

Christian Participation in Funeral Rituals

Like the marriage ceremony, the traditional funeral ritual takes precedence over Western-style, Christian rites. Since death is the most crucial event in the community and funeral rituals are among the most important to be performed, and since death brings everyone to a direct confrontation with the invisible spiritual world, it is the most critical point of contact between Christianity and traditional belief. It is interesting, then, to see what role a Christian pastor is able to find at such a time. The following case occurred in Kinshasa-Kalamu, just a few months before I left for Jerusalem in 1973.

Diangindu Jacques was born in the village of Mbanza-Baka, Republic of Congo, but grew up a few miles away in Banza-Lele, Kivunda district, in Zaire. He was raised as a Christian and attended elementary schools at Kimwanza (two years) and Banza-Lele (three years). When he was nineteen, and having graduated from Banza-Lele, he failed the entrance examination at Sundi-Lutete, the most prestigious Protestant high school in the area. His failure proved that his future was not in school. In fact, his secret ambition was to be a welder.

Since he was an active Christian, Banza-Lele Christians offered him the job of *nlongi a vata,* catechist of the Protestant church in Banza-Lele. To everyone's surprise, he declined the offer. His refusal frustrated his Christian parents, who then asked him to leave and build his own house. He obeyed and built his small house, but refused to get married. It seemed that his future was nowhere but in the village.

Two years later, however, his cousin Paul, a wealthy individual living in Dolisie, Congo Republic, decided to move to Kinshasa, Zaire. Jacques, who previously had no relatives in Kinshasa, left Banza-Lele for Kinshasa in search of work, coming to live with cousin Paul. Paul was so fond of him that he provided Jacques with everything he needed. From poverty, Jacques rose to a life of abundance with Paul's help. Moreover, his new social status did not weaken his Christian faith; he remained loyal and went to church every week. Within a few months he had become good friends with the pastor, in whose home he could come and go as he wished.

Although he had money, good clothes, and a well-furnished room, his heart was still in his desire to become a welder. So he started attending a vocational school, and unlike his previous experience with schooling in Banza-Lele, he proved to be a good student. The combination of his good character and quick learning made his teachers proud of him. He rarely missed classes and always did his assignments.

Suddenly one day after school he complained of having a severe headache. He took aspirin but did not feel better. He took some more and went to bed. Around 4:00 A.M. he became so ill that Paul took him to Clinique Danoise in Kinshasa-Gombe, considered at that time perhaps the best hospital in the city. He was hospitalized and treated by the best doctors. But around 5:00 A.M. on that same day, Jacques died. His death shocked everyone who knew him (including me, for we were good friends). People came from every corner of Kinshasa; some even came on foot from as far as Kimbanseke, more than twenty-five miles from where Jacques lived. His pastor came, too. But despite Jacques's devotion to Christianity, the pastor was just another individual in the crowd, not allowed to take charge of the funeral or even to play a significant role. The entire evening was devoted to traditional funeral activities, until finally, at midnight, Jacques's father asked the crowd to be quiet and give a few minutes to Jacques's best friend, the pastor, to say a few words. The pastor read the Twenty-Third Psalm and gave a resounding testimony on Jacques's earthly life. He assured the crowd that Jacques was saved and resting in Jesus' hands. Without this intervention by Jacques's father, the pastor would not have spoken a word that night.

Then, as the pastor was returning to his seat, a fight broke out between Jacques's paternal uncle and his maternal cousin. The paternal uncle claimed that Jacques had been "eaten" by Paul, Jacques's cousin and guardian, in order to make more money for himself. Other members of the two families soon became involved in the fight. Considerable effort was expended by other persons in the crowd to restore order. However, during all of this commotion the role of the pastor was nil. He could not say anything because he knew that nobody would listen; he had no authority here. He could even endanger his life with his Christian message.

A few hours before the body of Jacques was to be carried to the cemetery, the pastor privately consulted with the family and suggested to some of the most influential members of the kanda that they bring the body to the church before going to the cemetery. Although some of them regularly attended religious services, they refused to allow a Christian funeral. The pastor was frustrated, but could do nothing. He left unnoticed and did not accompany the body to the cemetery.

Even when a family accepts a Christian burial, the amount of time spent at the church and the cemetery (about two hours) is insignificant. It takes three days in villages and two days in cities for the traditional burial. The reason a Christian funeral is still meaningless among BaManianga as well as other African groups is that Christianity is regarded as a white man's religion. Until Christianity changes its image in Manianga, as well as in Africa generally, the Christian pastor's role at a death will remain insignificant.

The Spirit's Survival of Bodily Death

BaManianga's understanding of how the individual survives death is quite similar to that of other cultures worldwide, as expressed, for example, by D. Z. Phillips in *Death and Immortality*:

> It [the body] can be thought of as the prison within which the soul is temporarily restricted, the house within which it is lodged for a time, or as the suit of clothes which adorns a person for the

moment. The essence of a person, what it means to be a person, is identifiable with the mind or soul. This being so, it is argued, it is not surprising that at the dissolution of the body, the mind or soul should continue to exist, free at last from its former restrictions. It is all-important to this point of view to insist that "I" can be identified with one's mind or soul. Thus, the departed souls really are the departed, not some mere remnant of them. If John Jones can be identified with his soul, then if John Jones's soul survives John Jones's death, John Jones has survived his death. Unless one's soul is oneself, its survival would be of no interest to one.[27]

In BaManianga philosophy, a living person consists of three basic elements: *nitu,* the physical, visible body, or "death-body," because it dies (the dead physical body in the grave becomes *kiubula*); *kini,* the invisible body, a shade or reflection of nitu, looking exactly like it (sometimes this invisible body may be seen as an apparition after someone's death); and *mwela,* soul, which has no bodily form. At death, when the visible nitu dies, kini and mwela exit from it to start their journey to the other world. Together they form the life-body, that which continues alive, as opposed to the death-body, which has been discarded and left behind.

Visible nitu ("death-body") is the most suffering member of the three. It stores up all kinds of foreign agents: bacteria, disease, food, weathers, injuries, misfortunes. The individual's life expectancy may be either lengthened or shortened according to how well or badly it adjusts to these invaders. When it dies, it becomes worthless and must be buried quickly before it decomposes. It has no chance of returning to life again.

Kini has eternal life because mwela never divorces it. It is the member that dictates a man's behavior. Before the death of a visible nitu, no one can see it, but after death it may *pamuna,* show itself to kin who may not yet be informed about what has happened. This experience occurred to me at the time my father died in Kiloubi, Congo Republic, about a hundred miles from home. I and my two brothers saw him pass through the house, then vanish. We did not know until many hours later that he had died at about the time we had seen him. We were later told that he had come back to say goodbye. Kini is the visible body of the other world. Although it exerts control over this world's visible nitu, nitu has no influence over it.

Mwela is the key to survival of both nitu and kini. Like kini, mwela is invisible. But unlike kini, it cannot be seen by any living being. It lives in and from itself, without any help from either nitu or kini. But without help from mwela, neither nitu nor kini can survive. Mwela is therefore the most important of the three, for it gives life to both of the others. At night it may briefly leave the other two members when they are relaxing in sleep. To avoid their awareness of its exit, its activities at this time are reflected to them in dreams. If it should leave without returning, that would mean death. John S. Mbiti writes: "Death is recognized as the point when the spirit separates from the body. Because the spirit is closely associated with breathing, people know that the spirit (soul) has gone when a person stops breathing."[28] Mbiti's statement is also true for Manianga belief.

In a variation on the traditional Manianga beliefs that I gathered from my informants, Fukiau-kia-Bunseki, a Manianga scholar, states that mwela can separate not only from nitu at the time of death but also from kini. According to him, mwela goes away alone and separates from kanda and luvila (clan); that is, it seeks independence from social rules so that it can freely reincarnate in an about-to-be-born baby. He is not specific, however, as to how kini can remain apart from the element of soul, which is supposed to assure its continued existence.[29] Should his theory be right, would we still believe in life after death as a community of spiritual beings? What kind of existence could be attributed to the ancestors? Would we still claim that God continuously creates new human beings while those already created keep returning to this world? The world would not be able to feed all of us.

Indeed, BaManianga do believe in reincarnation, but this version of reincarnation is related, rather, to physical resemblance. A son may look, smile, talk, walk, and act like his father without having his father's mwela; otherwise, his father would not be alive, for he has only one mwela. It is not necessary to die before this physical resemblance can take place. And since this kind of reincarnation has to do only with physical resemblance, it is traditionally believed that the spirit of a dead person may continue to reincarnate itself in several generations to come. Reincarnation is not seen as a singly occurring event, but as a continuing trend.

The Total Spiritual Community of Living and Dead

Belief in the existence of the invisible, immortal kini and mwela provides the basis for the belief in the continuum of the kanda in the world beyond death. Beginning with the individual, the total community, like a series of concentric waves, spreads first into the members of the living community; then outward to the recent dead, who are in the process of becoming revered ancestors; and finally to those who have achieved the status of ancestors or little gods, who watch over, guide, and protect the community of the living. The community of the dead, Mpemba, includes all those who are on the way to becoming ancestors, those who have already reached that status, and those who may not become ancestors but who are however good spirits, such as children and those who may lack any desire to grow. And like the living community, Mpemba also has its outcasts.

The common name for the dead is nkuyu. But to make a clear distinction between the nkuyu who live at Mpemba and those who are not allowed to, the name *nkuyu* is generally reserved for those outcast from Mpemba. The residents of Mpemba are usually called *bakulu.*

Bankuyu (plural of *nkuyu*) are the evil dead who in their lifetime in this world were engaged in negative acts: kindoki, adultery, murder, theft, and all other major crimes. Because no one wants to deal with them, not much is known about the way they conduct their existence. The popular belief is that they do nothing but try to bother the living. Since they are excluded from living in Mpemba, they have no fixed place to stay. They are the nomads of the other world. Sometimes they return to their villages to disturb their living brothers. Consequently, to protect themselves against these unwanted visits, the living may take the drastic measure of planting pineapple trees, as earlier stated, all over the graves of those who are suspected of returning. This is the reason there are usually so many pineapple trees around the cemeteries, especially in the area where I was born. They may also pour poisonous magic medicine around the grave, although this must be done by nganga (priest). From the moment this is done, bankuyu, it is believed, will stop returning to torment their living relatives.

In the long term, bankuyu are believed to be transformed into *bisialala,* lizards. This belief is strengthened when one notices a lizard around a cemetery. This is their final destiny.

The ancestors, on the other hand, are the elders of the kanda in every imaginable way: chronologically, religiously, in intellect and in wisdom. Their name, *bakulu,* comes from the Kikongo verb *kula,* "to grow up." They are entitled to be respected, if not venerated.

To become an ancestor means more than simply being a resident of Mpemba or guardian of the kanda. Formerly I rejected the idea that Africans worship their ancestors. But I failed to respond objectively to the question "If indeed the ancestors are no more than guardians of the kanda, why are they foremost in people's day-to-day thinking and actions?" It became obvious that the only possibility of answering this question lay in a much deeper understanding of exactly what an "ancestor" is. To obtain such an understanding, one must return to the BaManianga interpretation of the first man Nzambi (God) created.

God created man, one will recall, to be his surrogate, or *alter sui.* In this role, man failed. But what he failed originally to be is precisely what the ancestors are now. To become an ancestor means to regain the status that the first man lost. Before death, we are just ordinary beings with no godlike status. But after death we find ourselves in the process of becoming God's surrogates, or little gods, namely, complete human beings. Humanness begins with God and extends to the ancestors. It has to do with the liberation of ordinary men from oppression, death, and bondage of the established human power. God created us to be free from human evil, to have dominion, power, and authority. Until BaManianga can claim to have this power, dominion, and authority, they are not yet human beings. But after being liberated from the oppression and evil of this world, the ancestors have power and authority, for they are now full human beings. Aware of their ancestors' complete humanness, BaManianga take the opportunity to surrender to them their day-to-day troubles because they (the ancestors) now possess authority to overcome human oppression. Using their power to improve the welfare of their living brothers, they become saviors and little gods for their particular relatives. Each ancestor's power is limited to his own kanda. Outside his kanda he does not intervene. Because of their liberating role, they deserve their people's respect, prayers, and veneration.

Though I am not advocating the idea of the ancestor "cult," I do not see why it must be considered idolatry if we worship ancestors. They are our little gods; their divinity—which in Kongo terms is their humanness—is directly related to the exercise of dominion. Therefore, to be an ancestor means to become as God originally intended Mahungu, the first man, to be: a little god, or God's *alter sui*. In this context, we can say that the ancestors are the new Mahungu. As far as I understand, Africans in general and BaManianga in particular believe that they have approval from God to venerate and worship their little gods in the same fashion that Christians worship Jesus Christ and saints. They are not prayed to in the Christian sense. People may pray to them just as they may pray to a tree, because through them God's spirit is revealed and felt.

Because of their power, authority, and dominion, ancestors are regarded as guardians of powerless and helpless human beings. They are the saviors of these hopeless beings. And some people regard these saviors as the Jesus of their particular makanda. In this sense, they believe, Jesus was already in Africa before Christianity arrived.

IV

GOD

The religious consciousness of BaManianga is not focused as restrictedly on God as it is in the Judeo-Christian tradition. In daily life, God is not called upon with appeals for help or protection, or invoked as a witness or a watchful presence. That level of interaction is instead assigned to the ancestors, who serve as God's intermediaries.

God's apparent detachment from day-to-day involvement in human affairs and the assumption of that role by the ancestors are explained mythically, as we have seen, in the story of Mahungu, the first human being. Mahungu was a complete being, a duplicate of God, containing both genders and possessing a knowledge of God's secrets. Because Mahungu proved to be irresponsible, God withdrew and allowed human beings to suffer without his constant attention and care. But taking pity on them, he brought them death, so they could return and, through desire and effort, gradually become like God again. Those who have reached that status are in effect the new Mahungu. They are complete or "grown-up" human beings: they have become "little gods." The term *ancestor* is reserved solely for this class of beings. Not everyone who has gone before can be called an ancestor. Ultimately, when ancestors lose their earthly existence completely, when no living being is able to remember them, and when their personality is no longer incarnated in newcomers, they are called *nkukunyungu:* light.

Because they are closer to God than we are, the ancestors are imbued with power and wisdom. And because they were once part of the human community, they can be used by God to project that power into daily life and circumstances. It is much easier for human beings to connect with the ancestors than it is to go directly to God. God made a place in the scheme of life for the ancestors so that human beings could maintain a connection and receive the blessings, wisdom, support, and correction emanating from God. The ancestors are God's servants.

God, as such, is indescribable. God is a power, like life itself, present in all things, even in the air we breathe. It would be impossible to describe God in words or to construct an intellectual concept of his nature. God can only be felt and perceived as all-pervasive power. There cannot be a material symbol of such power, or any location where that power is more present than at another. The power which contains all things cannot itself be contained.

Although the daily concerns of human beings are directed to the ancestors—the human representatives of God—it is also possible to address God directly through prayer. The word for prayer, *sambila,* in fact, is used exclusively for addressing God, and is not applied to communication with ancestors. Nzambi Mpungu, Nzambi Mpungu Mayanama, Mpungu Tulendo, and Mpungu Ngolo are the many names used to address God. A prayer can be made anywhere at any time, for God is always present. The notion of a church building or an altar where God's presence is concentrated or contained, an enclosed space especially suitable for prayer, is alien to Manianga thinking. People may pray at trees, rivers, or stones, not because there is a spirit in those things, but because the all-pervading power of God is there. Prayer when alone in natural, open places emphasizes the difference between personal prayer to God and the communal approach to ancestors. I was interested to find a remnant of this belief among African-Americans in the United States. A man I met in New Jersey told me that his grandmother in Alabama used to go to the forest to pray, because she felt that God was not confined to the church.

Prayer is the individual's approach to God, a way of expressing respect and humility, to ask for blessings, and to receive a sense of being strengthened by the sustaining presence of God. Prayer is completely personal. People never pray together or discuss the content of their prayers. Prayer is not a means of dealing with communal problems, for those fall under the jurisdiction of the ancestors. For example, a man would not pray to God to settle a dispute with a relative, for that would have to be negotiated by the community with ancestral guidance.

There have been rare occasions when the community, too, has addressed God directly. This has only happened as a response to a dire once-in-a-lifetime emergency such as a drought lasting several years and threatening to destroy the community. A group of women will go to the top of a hill, shout insults at God and bare their breasts, hoping to make him angry so he will act. This kind of action lies outside both prayer and communication with the ancestors, and is born out of desperation as a way to get God's attention. The ancestors would never be challenged in such a way, for they must always be treated respectfully.

The invisible world contains not only the ancestors but a multitude of other spirits. Most of them are benign, simply the spirits of men, women, and children who have departed this life. Some entities are evil and angry, however, and are capable of intruding upon the living just as readily as those who are dedicated to helping. A spirit is not merely a bodiless being, but is an active force. When a living person sees a spirit, he or she has, in effect, been taken into that spirit's mind. That is why one person in a group may experience a spirit's presence, while the others may not.

This occurred in my family in the late 1960s when I was attending high school in Kinshasa. A cousin of mine, Alphonse, a son of my father's sister, then about twenty-five years old, was walking on busy Boulevard du Trente Juin in the city when he suddenly saw my father standing in front of him. Alphonse had a special relationship with this uncle, for he had been named after him. My father appeared very happy and excited and began talking animatedly. He was well dressed in an expensively tailored suit, and explained that he now owned a number of stores and would like his nephew to visit him. Although my father had been dead for over ten years, Alphonse was so surprised that he did not think of that, but began to ask the address of the place where he could come to see him. Before he could finish, my father had vanished. The entire experience had lasted only a minute or two, and did not seem to be noticed by anyone passing by.

It had happened around noon during the lunch hour when the streets of Kinshasa were crowded. Alphonse showed other family members the exact spot, and for months afterward when I was not in school I would sometimes go to that place at noon hoping that my father would appear there again. Others in the family did the same. A sister even traveled from the village to see the spot where it happened. Alphonse was already a teenager when my father died and had known him well. He recognized him instantly. To our regret, the experience was never repeated.

The invisible world thus interacts constantly with the visible one, for both are part of the vast cosmological plan of life and death. For BaManianga, that design begins with the kanda, the community of this world, and extends outward like a series of concentric rings to the after-death world of spirits, then to the realm of the ancestors, or little gods, in a continuous, unbroken communal order. God is absent from this design, because he cannot be located. God is believed to be everywhere. God is therefore more than this plan and cannot be contained in it. God's power sustains all of life and is always acknowledged to be the real and ultimate power behind the ancestors and other spiritual beings and their actions.

EPILOGUE
Kongo Belief in Its Contemporary Setting

Any discussion of the nature and role of God in Kongo belief leads inevitably to a consideration of how the introduction of Christianity over the past three centuries has interacted with traditional beliefs. Manianga tradition has had to confront Christian influences at almost every point, whether to resist or to accept and adapt.

Generally speaking, Manianga Christians have not replaced traditional beliefs as much as they have simply supplemented them. Two modes of belief exist side by side and are assigned to different aspects of an individual's life, resulting in a dual outlook. This is evident in the tendency of Manianga Christians to accept two Gods, their traditional God and the God of the missionaries. The Christian God is worshiped on Sundays in church, because he is perceived as being limited and confined to buildings and designated times for worship. A cornerstone of Protestant missionary teaching was the evil of smoking and drinking. But people felt that God was watching them only when they were in his building. During the week, they thought, "We can drink or smoke as we please, because God is in the building and cannot see us."

The missionaries insisted that before they came, BaManianga did not worship God. But with their own well-developed idea of an unlimited, always-present God, it was difficult for BaManianga to understand how the Christian God could be different from their own. Of course, had Europeans accepted the fact that a universal God already existed in Manianga thinking, it would have legitimized Kongo belief and rendered their missionary work

138

unnecessary. A place therefore had to be found for this alien God. And with the emphasis on the church building and weekly meetings, which were not a part of traditional communal life, Christianity did not replace or modify existing belief as much as it occupied a newly created area. As we have seen, the important rituals of community life centering on birth, marriage, and death still take precedence today even among the most devout Christians and even among educated persons living in modern cities. The missionaries, with their habit of addressing all problems directly to God and positing an invisible world devoid of spirits and spirit forces, seemed to be impoverishing the rich and more complex spiritual universe of BaManianga, and therefore, as well, their psychological and communal lives, which were bound up in that universe. The custom of solitary prayer in the presence of any natural object, because God can be found anywhere, was condemned as praying to nature spirits. Communication with ancestors, God's servants and intermediaries, was mistakenly called an "ancestor cult," an unworthy substitute for worship of God. In both cases, the more elaborate cosmology and the differing concept of the human relation to God were misunderstood. The only exception to the Christian failure to capture traditional belief is the immense popularity of the figure of Jesus. This is because Jesus can be recognized in the role of nganga, prophète, and ancestor, and therefore fits readily into the system of Kongo cosmology.

Traditional systems of belief have proved to be extremely tenacious in Africa and resistant to basic change. This is due in large part to the fact that they are inseparable from communal life, more likely to adapt to new circumstances than to die out and be replaced. For they are needed in order to sustain the continued life of a deeply communal people. With the resurgence of pride and interest in their own traditions, Africans are becoming impatient with Western denigration of their religious cultures as "primitive" or inferior. Indeed, some African intellectuals charge that the miseries suffered by Africans can be attributed to their having accepted a white European God and alienated their own. When I was a student in the Department of Religion at the University of Zaire, Kisangani, our professor of African religions argued that the only way the African race will save itself from oppression, racism, and humiliation is to get rid of the imported God who is alien to African consciousness. A native of Zaire, he was an ordained Christian minister with a Th.D. degree from the Harvard Divinity School. I have heard similar remarks made by others, even jokingly and in a church setting.

Former Archbishop Milingo of Zambia, who was removed from his position and disciplined by the Vatican for bringing African rituals of healing and fighting of evil spirits into his charismatic work, has eloquently stated the enduring nature of African tradition in the face of unrelenting white condemnation and assumptions of superiority:

> They [the Europeans] have come to teach Africans accepted gestures, movements, and drums. What they approve, we Africans must approve. What they do not like, we must give up. They have gone so far as to incite the Africans themselves to condemn their own traditional values supposed to be included in the liturgy. The principle to guide them is that there is nothing pure and sacred in all that is African; they pose before us as the sacred and the pure, having the spirit of discernment for genuine African values worthy to be included in the liturgy. Our Africanness is with us and in us. We have been fed on it and brought up on it.[1]

Traditional Kongo belief endures because it envisions a world constantly seeking a timeless peace and equilibrium. Human life is not seen as rushing headlong through linear history toward death, on a collision course with itself. It is not perceived as a life-or-death battle between good and evil, with the hope that the good may someday totally win, perhaps at an Armageddon. Instead, human beings are accepted as imperfect; forgiveness is more important than punishment. The social order has its roots in the invisible world. Evils endlessly arise and must be dealt with wisely, so that the prosperity and mutual good will of the community can continue always to thrive. Life is like the sea, with the restless and interminable rise and fall of the waves, even though the level stays the same. God is the power of life. Human beings must allow themselves to be guided by the most seasoned and experienced human wisdom, crystallized in the ancestors, who timelessly watch over our lives, ready to chastise or encourage.

Africans by nature are optimistic. Tomorrow, we say, will be better than our yesterdays.

Appendix

Kikongo Texts

"Let us go see the cross . . ."

Twenda tadi kulunsi
Diatufwila Yesu
Vana vena Mvulusi
Beto katufwila

Kulunsi, kulunsi
Diatufwila Yesu
Zola diau tuna sa
Nzanu miena yeto

Vana kakwamuswa
Bukakutufwila
Zola kweti monika
Kuna kwa Kinzambi

Va kulunsi Mvulusi
Wasa fotikisa
Ntu a Satana nade
Ye wanziona ngolo

Vana ndiamu Satana
Kiadi kiena yandi
Bukamona Mvulusi
Ye Zimbasi zandi

"Forgive us coming . . ."

Lutusila nlemvo mu kwiza
Kulubumina mu ntangu ya mpilayayi
Batata ba lwatusisila bubote mpia
Mpasi zibaseki
Bibunda fwa
Buna beto bana kiadi kiseki
Mu mona luzingu lwa batata

Vo bau beti tatamana fwa
Buna banani tufweti bundila
Diaka ntulu?
Mu manisa mpasi zozo
Buna beto bana butulele o bwabu:
Mbazi batata babo
Bayenda mu zimbanza
Basala ku bwala
Bafweti kukusa
Nwiza nwakututadisa
Wonso usanga bobo
Nzengolo andi lufwa.

"As I am chief of this village . . ."

Bu ngiena mfumu a vata diadi
Buna babingi bakumbanzilanga
Vo yi ndoki
Bwabu ntelamane va kulunsi diadi
Beno bayaya ku Makulu
Vo yi ndoki
Vo ya dia muntu
Buna yinsuka yi
Tamana vutukila
Buna mfutu ami lufwa.

"In the name of the Father . . ."

Mu nkumbu a Se ye Mwana ye Mpeve yanlongo ngieti fukama va
ntadisi a beno zintumwa za Yesu mu lomba nlemvo mu mambu
mamonsono malembolo fwanana mamvengi mu lumbu ki. Lukun-
demvukila mpasi vo ntim'ami wakala nampwe bonso mvula zampembe.

"I am pleased to see you all . . ."

Ntondele mu kulumona babo
Tekila nkwendolo ami kwa bayaya
Ntomene zaya bu lwenina mu lokula kiaki
Kansi ngieti kululomba mu lembo sakisa kiadi

Lutatamana zolasana
Lutatamana keba ntoto watusisila bayaya
Ka teka ko
Nanga vena ye muntu mu beno ye bankaka mpe
Wabele lembo kunzolanga
Kandemvukila mu lokula kiaki
Mono kivwidi muntu bila ko
Ntim'ami wakia nadede
Kiena nkutu ye kiadi ko mu kwenda landi bayaya
Kalusakisi kiadi ko kadi tuna monana kweto diaka.

"It is now time for me to go . . ."

Bwabu mono si yi kwenda
Kanda (moyo) diadi
Nge kusole wankuntu
Nge kusole wanleke
Babonsono bantu baku
Mioyo buna miena
Miamio miaku
Kanda (moyo) disidi naku
Kionso kilubeki lukabana
Yala wazinga, wasala mbongo
Bibusi ye bampangi badia zo
Ah tu . . . tu

"We strangers, we travelers . . ."

Beto banzenza, minkibi kaka
Mu ntoto wau wamviokila
Ye bisi kanda yeto nsi.

Nsi eto yena mu nza yamona
Mu nza yalunga ya Mvulusi
Zimpasi meni, mansanga nkatu
Mayangi kaka mu yoyo nsi.

Se, Yesu Klisto wateka kwenda
Mu tunga nzo yituvwandila
Mu lamba ndambisa kwa bayandi
Mu kubavwika mianzitusu.

Babo banlongo bameni nunga
Bameni kota mu mvundulu
Bavingilanga mu kutukika
Mu kiese kio kia mvu ya mvu.

Mu kiese kiokio tuvilakana
Mamo ma mpasi ma ntangu yi
Matwalembana tuna vanga
Mamo maswekwa twazaya mo.

Mvwatu miampembe, kolwa kiamoyo
Nkumbu zamona, biabio biampa
Ye mu mamonsono tuna mona
Se dieto Nzambi ye fwanana.

"O father, I am supported . . ."

O tata mono yayekama
Mu zaku ngolo ye diami se
O mayangi Mfumu ami ye Nzambi ami
Tuta Aleluya Mvulusi.
E e mayangi tuta
A aleluya e e ntinu a dizulu
Udumanga yala kaka ke yalanga
Mfumu ami ye Nzambi ami.

"Father, do not be surprised . . ."

Tata kuyituku ko vo twizidi kutala
Mu kinsweki. Tuka wakutusisidi
Buna mpasi bwatela mpia. Nanga mpe ngeye
Mosi tomene zaya bonso bwayikidi
Luzingu lweto. Lumbu kiokio kitwayiza
Kufila kwaku yi lumbu kiokio mpe twakulwa
Mu nzo. Tata Makonko wayikidi yo duminanga
Nzo aku bwabu. Yandi vo mu ntangu yiwakele
Moyo twakele vovanga, bwabu i tour andi
Mu vova. Bima biabio biwatusisila nate ye
Mbongo zabeto kibeni zitwakele kwe lundingi
Zakamana tambula. Ka twayenda ye kima ko
Ku vata dia mama. Ye landila bonso twakele
Vwezilanga kanda dia mama buna.

Twayikidi kweto bisakununu nadede
Bankaka nkutu nkumbu beti kutubokidilanga
Yi mazoba. Vo yi mu batata babakento nga
Nanga twakinu kweto mu nzo eto. Kansi
Batata babakaka bu batelama buna
Nzengolo au vo twavayika kaka
Dila kweto twekwedidingi kadi
Kinsona kitu sakidi tuka watusisidi
Mama wasala kwa yandi kaka
Wakutu tatukwa kwa mbamba . . .

"As I cannot return . . ."

Bu kina vo kilendi vutuka manima ko buna ngeye mwan'ami
wambuta fwetisisa bwabu skulu ye sosa kisalu kia mundele. Mu
tombuka mu nswalu buna fweti sosa kisalu kia teka mu makazini.
Toma zaya vo mpasi una mona sungulako ku mbadukulu bu
wakinu kaka fi mwana. Kansi kulendi mona wonga nkutu ko kadi
mono ngina kala yaku ntangu zazo. Kina kusisa nkutu ko. Yi ngeye
bwabu weka mfumu a nzo. Ndekele dio minu vo mpangi zaku
bana baka lusadusu lwafwana mu manisi kalasi biau.

"I do not have much to tell you . . ."

Ka Kien' ami mamingi mu kusonga ko
Ngieti kaka kuzodila ngiendolo yambote kwa bayaya
Bwabu butweka mu vambana yaku buna ntim'ami ufulukidi kwa
Kiadi kikondolo tezo. Kiadi kiakingi kiena yami
Ka bweyi diaka mfweti vanga? Maza matiamukini matiamukini kaka.
Kizeyi ko vo ngina nunga mu bangula kwa bana vo kabalendi ku mona
diaka ko.
Koko kuweti kwenda kutuvilakane ko. Bonso butweti kubanza yi bo.
Wakutubanzanga beto mpe. Vuvu kiami vo tuna monana kweto diaka.
Vo lufwa lwalu kwa Nzambi lutukidi ka diambu ko,
Kansi vo kwa nkwa bumfunia lutukidi buna ukunlanda ka lembo baka,
Mpongoso mu mwel'andi
Wenda mu yenge . . .

NOTES

Preface

1. Albert J. Raboteau, *Slave Religion* (New York: Oxford University Press, 1978), pp. 4–5.
2. Ibid., p. 7.

One. The Spirituality of a Communal People

1. Ferdinand Ngoma, "L'Initiation Ba-Kongo et sa signification" (Thèse de doctorat, 3ᵉ Cycle, Université de Paris, 1963), p. 17.
2. Conversations with Duki (Chief) Mabwaka, 1972.
3. John M. Janzen, *The Quest for Therapy in Lower Zaire* (Berkeley: University of California Press, 1978), pp. 11–12.
4. Henry Morton Stanley, *The Congo*, vol. 1 (London: Sampson Low and Co., 1885), pp. 281–82.
5. John M. Janzen, "A Lower-Congo Example of the Regional Council as a Micropolity," paper presented at the African Studies Association's Tenth Annual Meeting, November 1–4, 1967, New York, p. 6.
6. Georges Balandier, *The Sociology of Black Africa* (New York: Praeger, 1970), p. 153.
7. Popular song among Kongo-Ndibu of Luidi.
8. Wesley H. Brown, "Marriage Payment: A Problem in Christian Social Ethics among Kongo Protestants" (Ph.D. dissertation, University of Southern California, 1971), p. 34.
9. Julius K. Nyerere, *Ujamaa-Essays on Socialism* (London: Oxford University Press, 1968), p. 93.
10. John S. Mbiti, *African Religions and Philosophy* (London: Heinemann, 1969), p. 108.
11. Ngoma, "L'Initiation Ba-Kongo," p. 24.
12. J. van Wing, *Etudes Bakongo* (Bruges: Desclée de Brouwer, 1959), p. 85. My translation differs slightly from Balandier's in *Sociology of Black Africa,* p. 299.
13. Batsikama ba Mampuya is the first Manianga to suggest that BaKongo became matrilineal by necessity. As the father was unable to feed his children, the mother worked hard to secure the survival of her children. When she left her husband's kanda, she took her children with her. From R. Batsikama ba Mampuya ma Ndwala, *Voici les Jagas ou l'histoire d'un peuple parricide bien malgré lui* (Kinshasa: O.N.R.D., 1971), p. 244.
14. Ngoma, "L'Initiation Ba-Kongo," p. 16. He gives a more detailed list of Kongo meanings on this page.
15. Batsikama, *Voici les Jagas,* p. 241.

16. Ngoma, "L'Initiation Ba-Kongo." He describes his own case when he was traveling in an unknown region. He met brothers and sisters he never knew before, who helped him in every way. As a result he saved all his money.

17. *Bandoki* are excluded.

18. Balandier, *Sociology of Black Africa,* p. 300.

19. Ibid., p. 201.

20. Ngoma, "L'Initiation Ba-Kongo," p. 28.

21. De Gleene; quoted in Wyatt MacGaffey in *Custom and Government in the Lower Congo* (Berkeley: University of California Press, 1970), p. 262.

22. Balandier, *Sociology of Black Africa,* p. 320.

23. Van Wing, *Etudes,* p. 133.

24. Agnes C. Donohugh, "Essentials of African Culture," *Africa* 8, no. 3 (1935), p. 330.

25. Larry Dossey, *Meaning and Medicine* (New York: Bantam, 1991), p. 60.

26. Oral tradition.

27. Bahelele Ndimisina, *Lusansu ya Fu bia N'Kongo ku Bas-Zaire tekila 1900* (Kinshasa: Centre Protestant d'Editions et de Diffusion, 1977), p. 13.

28. Benjamin C. Ray, *African Religions* (Englewood Cliffs, N.J.: Prentice-Hall, 1976), p. 132.

29. Ibid., pp. 132–33.

30. Henri A. Junod, *The Life of a South African Tribe,* vol. 1 (New Hyde Park, N.Y.: University Books, 1962), p. 436.

Two. The Communal Response to Death and Misfortune

1. I prefer to use the verb *to fashion* rather than *to create* to avoid misunderstanding BaManianga's idea of creation, namely, that God did not create ex nihilo as the Bible claims.

2. Some Manianga Christians interpret Jesus as a "born-again" Mahungu. As a result they believe that Christianity did not bring Jesus to Africa, for he was already there under African names.

3. Thomas Louis Vincent, *La Mort africaine: Idéologie funéraire en Afrique noire* (Paris: Payot, 1982), p. 27.

4. Edward E. Evans-Pritchard, *Witchcraft, Oracles and Magic among the Azande* (Oxford: Clarendon Press, 1958), p. 21.

5. Buakasa Tulu kia Mpansu, "Le Discours de la kindoki ou sorcellerie," *Cahiers des Religions Africaines* 4, no. 11 (1972), p. 29.

6. A fictitious name to avoid disparaging any important person.

7. Jean Masamba, "Psychotherapeutic Dynamics in African Bewitched Patients: Toward a Multidimensional Therapy in Social Psychiatry" (Th.D. dissertation, School of Theology at Claremont, 1972), p. 51.

8. Ibid., pp. 51–52.

9. Conversations with Chief Malonga, Banza-Lele, July 1972.

10. M. G. Marwick, *Sorcery in Its Social Setting* (Manchester: Manchester University Press, 1965), p. 147.

11. Brown, "Marriage Payment," p. 37.

12. Ibid., pp. 37–38.

13. Evans-Pritchard, *Witchcraft*, pp. 124–25.

14. As a child I often went to Tadi (the most important commercial center in the area) with my parents. Surprisingly, I was always forbidden to enter Muzenge's store. As I can recall it today, his store was always empty. His name has been changed here to protect his identity. If he is still alive he must be very old and may no longer own that store.

15. Efraim Andersson, *Messianic Popular Movements in the Lower Congo* (Studia Ethnographica Upsaliensa XIV, 1958), p. 201.

16. Recorded as told to me by Chief Mabwaka, Banza-Lele, November 1972.

17. Andersson, *Messianic Popular Movements*, p. 201.

18. Ibid., pp. 202–3.

19. Jonas Masamba, a key member of the Kikwimba clan-section (Banza-Lele).

20. *Minkunga mia Kintwadi* (Union Hymnal), no. 167.

21. This address was delivered by ya Binsuka. As I could not return to Zaire to have him record what he had said, I sent a blank tape to my brother, who taped it for me. Since the speech originally took place in 1953, there may be a slight change between what he said at that time and what he said for my work. However, I believe that this change (if it exists) must have been minimal.

22. Reverend Makanzu, mimeographed as reported in John M. Janzen and Wyatt MacGaffey, eds., *An Anthology of Kongo Religion* (University of Kansas Publications in Anthropology 5, 1974), p. 85.

23. See also Evans-Pritchard, *Witchcraft*, pp. 40f.

24. B. Hallen and J. O. Sodipo, *Knowledge, Belief and Witchcraft* (London: Ethnographia, 1986), p. 94.

25. Wyatt MacGaffey, *Religion and Society in Central Africa: The BaKongo of Lower Zaire* (Chicago: University of Chicago Press, 1986), p. 165.

26. No one is sure that this mysterious stuff indeed comes from the dead.

27. Kiantandu Mavumi-sa, mimeographed (National University of Zaire, Kisangani, June 1972).

28. Konda Jean, as reported in Janzen and MacGaffey, eds., *Anthology of Kongo Religion*, p. 5.

29. Karl E. Laman, *Dictionnaire Kikongo-Français*, vol. 2, p. 761.

30. Beth Elverdam, "Where Men and Women Have Separate Worlds: How Ritual Is Used as a Mechanism of Socialization," *Temenos* 13 (1977), p. 59.

31. Ray, *African Religions*, p. 91.

32. BaManianga consider Kinkimba a school, not a simple rite.

33. *Mungwala* means a neophyte who never attended Kinkimba. Any

time the nkimba went for a walk, they were to cry out, *"Ciorr, ciorr, ciorr,"* a warning to mangwala who might happen to be in the vicinity to hide. In turn, when mangwala were in the Kinkimba neighborhood, the law requested them to cry, *"Mono uwu* (It is I)," a warning that nkimba should hide. Otherwise, if they saw the nkimba because of remaining silent, they were to be prosecuted. The fine could be a human being: the offender would give up a slave to the offended. The same fine could be imposed upon the nkimba if they were seen because of not hiding or crying out. It was two-way justice. It should be noted that the official language of Kinkimba is not an original one but is based linguistically on Kikongo. All Kongo people, whether in Lower Zaire, Angola, or the Congo Republic, speak only one language: Kikongo. It is my belief that it was invented to equal the Catholics who used Latin in their seminaries. Reverend Bahelele suggests that Kinkimba did not exist before the coming of Christianity to the Kongo. The language was very strange, as already stated. Here are some sentences of that language, followed by their Kikongo equivalents: (1) Nzibwa ngebwa? (Nkumbu aku nanie, What is your name?); (2) Kwa bungweni tu fumukini? (Kwe tukidie, Where are you coming from?); (3) Ngononuntu fumukini kunziala wangono mwa (Mono ntukidi ku nzo ami, I am coming from home); (4) Nimva se ngebo (Nayendi kwaku, Go in peace; literally, You can go now); (5) Zidi ezo? (Ka Bwakoe? Isn't it?); (6) Kweze (Inga, ingeta, yes).

34. I am indebted to Reverend Bahelele for his mimeograph, "Lusansu ye Fu bia N'Kongo tekila 1900," which he gladly allowed me to read during a retreat of Evangelical Church ministers at Kibunzi Mission in July 1971.

35. Mahaniah Kimpianga, *La Maladie et la guérison en milieu Kongo* (Kinshasa: EDICVA, Département de la Recherche, Centre de Vulgarisation Agricole, 1982), p. 97.

36. Carl G. Jung, *Aion,* in *Collected Works,* vol. 9, pt. 2, Bollingen Series XX (Princeton: Princeton University Press, 1979), p. 86.

Three. The Concept of Death

1. Edmond Mujynya, "Le Mystère de la mort dans le monde bantu," *Cahiers des Religions Africaines* 5, no. 3 (1969), p. 25.

2. The first time he told me the story, I was so overwhelmed with fear and emotion that I could neither record nor write it down. Every time I did something he did not like, he talked about his death. Finally, I became bored and did not want to hear it again. However, when his second death was revealed, I was afraid to lose him. I had about fifty zaires (100 U.S. dollars) at the time and decided to buy a tape recorder. It cost me about thirty-five zaires. As soon as I got it, I rushed to his house and asked him to tape the story of his first death. Though I did not care much at that time about his story, I decided to formally interview him for two reasons: first, if he should die (and he did die a year later) I would

still be able to hear his voice; and second, knowing that his beloved story had been taped, he would die happier.

3. After returning to this world, tata Bethuel became a charismatic Christian, devoting his time and money to Jesus' cause, without however breaking with the traditional beliefs in which he was raised. He remained faithful to both Christianty and tradition.

4. As her last name was identical to the family name of Pope Paul VI, she became a more devoted Catholic than ever after his election to the papacy.

5. She gave me the impression that this "Abraham" was the Biblical ancestor of Christians, Jews, and Muslims. "Peter" was certainly the New Testament disciple.

6. J. Decapmaeker, "Les Funérailles chez les Bakongo," *Aequatoria* 14, no. 3 (1951), p. 81.

7. Ibid.

8. Oral tradition.

9. It is important to note that his wife and children are traditionally excluded from inheriting his fortune because they are not members of his kanda. This custom, however, is under heavy criticism mostly from townsmen and intellectuals, and in many parts of Manianga it is now only a living memory.

10. Simon Mfuka, "La Théologie traditionelle des BaManianga" (Mémoire de license, National University of Zaire, Kisangani, 1973), with some addenda, p. 48.

11. Junod, *Life of a South African Tribe,* vol. 1, p. 143.

12. Ray, *African Religions,* p. 141.

13. A. R. Radcliffe-Brown, *The Andaman Islanders* (Glencoe, Ill.: Free Press, 1964), p. 258.

14. Jack Goody, *Death, Property and the Ancestors* (Stanford, Calif.: Stanford University Press, 1962), p. 125.

15. MacGaffey, *Custom and Government,* p. 162.

16. Ibid., p. 150.

17. The question of bitheism among Manianga Christians (and other African Christians) has never been raised because not every Christian is aware of believing in two different Gods. The root of this bitheism is the missionaries. Importing their Christian God to Africa, they failed to understand that the same God was already there. And since they introduced him to Africans as a Westerner rather than a universal God, the Africans in general and BaManianga in particular regard him as the missionaries' God. They therefore believe in two different Gods who, in their understanding, are not quite the same.

18. *Minkunga mia Kintwadi* (Union Hymnal) no. 745. The last sentence refers to the original status of the first created human being before his fall. They believe that through death this status will be regained.

19. MacGaffey, *Custom and Government,* pp. 162–64.

20. For BaManianga, it is taboo to see the sexual organs of a person who is not of one's gender or generation. It is all right for friends,

brothers, or sisters to take baths together, but it is a sin for father and son to do this, for they do not belong to the same generation.
21. Decapmaeker, "Funérailles," p. 82.
22. Goody (*Death, Property and the Ancestors,* p. 131) notices the same thing among the LoDagaa.
23. Van Wing, *Etudes,* p. 53.
24. Jean Buxton, *Religion and Healing in Mandari* (Oxford: Clarendon Press, 1973), p. 149.
25. Ibid., p. 146.
26. Other makanda still exclude the deceased's children and widow from taking part in the distribution.
27. D. Z. Phillips, *Death and Immortality* (London: Macmillan, 1970), pp. 3–4.
28. John S. Mbiti, *Introduction to African Religion* (London: Heinemann, 1975), pp. 118–19.
29. L. Fukiau-kia-Bunseki, "Kindoki ou Solution attendue" (unpublished essay, 1968), p. 13.

Epilogue

1. E. Milingo, *The World in Between: Christian Healing and the Struggle for Spiritual Survival* (Maryknoll, N.Y.: Orbis, 1984), p. 73.

SELECTED BIBLIOGRAPHY

Andersson, Efraim. *Churches at Grass-Roots*. London: Lutterworth, 1968.
———. *Messianic Popular Movements in the Lower Congo*. Studia Ethnographia Upsaliensa XIV, 1958.
Bahelele Ndimisina. *Lusansu ya Fu bia N'Kongo ku Bas-Zaire tekila 1900* (Culture and customs of N'Kongo prior to 1900). Kinshasa: Centre Protestant d'Editions et de Diffusion, 1977.
Balandier, Georges. *Daily Life in the Kingdom of the Kongo*. London: George Allen & Unwin, 1968.
———. *Sociologie actuelle de l'Afrique noire*. Paris: Presses Universitaires de France, 1963.
———. *The Sociology of Black Africa*. New York: Praeger, 1970.
Batsikama ba Mampuya ma Ndwala, R. *Voici les Jagas ou l'histoire d'un peuple parricide bien malgré lui*. Kinshasa: O.N.R.D., 1971.
Bond, George, Walton Johnson, and Sheila S. Walker. *African Christianity*. New York: Academic Press, 1979.
Bongeye Senza Masa. "The Life of the Church," *All Africa Conference of Churches* 10, no. 3 (no date): 16–18, 23.
Brown, Wesley H. "Marriage Payment: A Problem in Christian Social Ethics among Kongo Protestants." Ph.D. dissertation, University of Southern California, 1971.
Buakasa Tulu kia Mpansu. "Le Discours de la kindoki ou sorcellerie," *Cahiers des Religions Africaines* 4, no. 11 (1972): 5–67.
Buhlmann, Walbert. *The Missions on Trial*. Maryknoll, N.Y.: Orbis, 1979.
Buxton, Jean. *Religion and Healing in Mandari*. Oxford: Clarendon Press, 1973.
Cone, James H. *God of the Oppressed*. New York: Seabury, 1975.
Cuvelier, J. *L'Ancien royaume de Congo*. Bruges: Desclée de Brouwer, 1946.
Decapmaeker, J. "Les Funérailles chez les Bakongo," *Aequatoria* 14, no. 3 (1951): 81–84; no. 4 (1951): 125–28.
Dimomfu, Lapika. "L'Art de guérir chez les Kongo du Zaire: Discours magique ou science médicale? *Cahiers du CEDAF*, no. 3, May 1984. Brussels: Centre d'Etude de Documentation Africaines, 1984.
Donohugh, Agnes C. "Essentials of African Culture," *Africa* 8, no. 3 (1935): 329–39.
Dossey, Larry. *Meaning and Medicine*. New York: Bantam, 1991.
Elverdam, Beth. "Where Men and Women Have Separate Worlds: How Ritual Is Used as a Mechanism of Socialization," *Temenos* 13 (1977): 56–67.
Evans-Pritchard, Edward E. *Witchcraft, Oracles and Magic among the Azande*. Oxford: Clarendon Press, 1958.

Fukiau-kia-Bunseki, Lumanisa. *N'Kongo ye Nza yakun'zungidila.* Kinshasa, 1969.

———. "Kindoki ou solution attendue." Unpublished essay. Luyalungunu lwa Kumba, 1968.

Goody, Jack. *Death, Property and the Ancestors.* Stanford, Calif.: Stanford University Press, 1962.

Gregor, Arthur S. *Witchcraft and Magic.* New York: Scribners, 1972.

Hallen, Barry. *Knowledge, Belief and Witchcraft: Analytic Experiments in African Philosophy.* London: Ethnographica, 1986.

Haule, Cosmos. *Bantu Witchcraft and Christian Morality.* Nouvelle Revue de Science Missionaire, 1969.

Janzen, John M. "Elemental Categories, Symbols, and Ideas of Association in Kongo-Manianga Society," Ph.D. dissertation, University of Chicago, 1967.

———. *The Quest for Therapy in Lower Zaire.* Berkeley: University of California Press, 1978.

———. "A Lower-Congo Example of the Regional Council as a Micropolity," paper presented at the African Studies Association's Tenth Annual Meeting, November 1–4, New York, 1967.

———, and Wyatt MacGaffey, eds. *An Anthology of African Religion.* University of Kansas Publications in Anthropology 5, 1974.

Jung, Carl G. *Aion. Collected Works,* vol. 9, pt. 2. Bollingen Series XX. Princeton: Princeton University Press, 1979.

Junod, Henri A. *The Life of a South African Tribe.* 2 vols. New Hyde Park, N.Y.: University Books, 1962.

Kiantandu, Mavumisa. "Les Morts-vivants, la kindoki et le kinganga chez les Bakongo." Paper presented at the National University of Zaire, Kisangani, June 1972.

Kraft, Charles H. *Christianity in Culture.* Maryknoll, N.Y.: Orbis, 1979.

Laman, Karl E. *Dictionnaire Kikongo-Français.* Brussels: Institut Royal Colonial Belge, 1932.

MacGaffey, Wyatt. *Custom and Government in the Lower Congo.* Berkeley: University of California Press, 1970.

———. *Modern Kongo Prophets.* Bloomington: Indiana University Press, 1983.

———. *Religion and Society in Central Africa: The BaKongo of Lower Zaire.* Chicago: University of Chicago Press, 1986.

———, ed. and trans. *Art and Healing of the BaKongo Commented on by Themselves: Minkisi from the Laman Collection.* Stockholm: Folkens Museum-Etnografiska, 1991.

MacGavran, Donald A., and Norman Riddle. *Zaire: Midday in Missions.* Valley Forge, Pa.: Judson, 1979.

McVeigh, Malcolm J. *God in Africa.* Cape Cod, Mass.: Claude Stark, 1974.

Mahaniah Kimpianga. *La Mort dans la pensée Kongo.* Kisantu, Zaire: Centre de Vulgarisation Agricole, 1980.

———. *La Maladie et la guérison en milieu Kongo.* Kinshasa: EDICVA; Département de la Recherche, Centre de Vulgarisation Agricole, 1982.

Marwick, M. G. *Sorcery in Its Social Setting.* Manchester: Manchester University Press, 1965.

Masamba, Jean. "Psychotherapeutic Dynamics in African Bewitched Patients: Toward a Multidimensional Therapy in Social Psychiatry." Th.D. dissertation, School of Theology at Claremont, 1972.

Mbiti, John S. *African Religions and Philosophy.* London: Heinemann, 1969.

———. *Concepts of God in Africa.* London: S.P.C.K., 1970.

———. "The Encounter between Christianity and African Religion," *Temenos* 12 (1977): 125–35.

———. *Introduction to African Religion.* London: Heinemann, 1975.

———. *The Prayers of African Religion.* Maryknoll, N.Y.: Orbis, 1975.

———, ed. *African and Asian Contributions to Contemporary Theology.* Chateau de Bossey, Switzerland: Ecumenical Institute, June 1976.

Mendelsohn, Jack. *God, Allah and JuJu.* Boston: Beacon, 1962.

Mfuka, Simon. "La Théologie traditionelle des BaManianga," Mémoire de license (thesis), National University of Zaire, Kisangani, 1973.

Milingo, E. *The World in Between: Christian Healing and the Struggle for Spiritual Survival.* Maryknoll, N.Y.: Orbis, 1984.

Mort, funérailles, deuil et culte des ancêtres chez les populations du Kwango/Bas-Kwili. Centre d'Etudes Ethnologiques, Series I, vol. 3, 1969.

Mujynya, Edmond. "Le Mystère de la mort dans le monde bantu," *Cahiers des Religions Africaines* 5, no. 3 (1969): 25–35.

Nadel, S. F. "Witchcraft and Anti-Witchcraft in Nupe Society," *Africa* 8, no. 4 (1935): 324–445.

Ngoma, Ferdinand. *L'Initiation Ba-Kongo et sa signification.* Centre d'Etude des Problèmes Sociaux Indigènes, Collection de Mémoires, 1963.

Nyerere, Julius K. *Ujamaa-Essays on Socialism.* London: Oxford University Press, 1968.

Nzolani, R. "Kindoki kiena kiakedika" (Kindoki is real). Unpublished essay. Luyalungunu lwa Kumba, 1966.

Oberg, Kalervo. "Kinship Organization of the Banyakole," *Africa* 11, no. 2 (1938): 128–58.

Parrinder, Geoffrey. *African Traditional Religion.* London: Sheldon, 1974.

Perrin, Marie-France J. *Basic Community in the African Churches.* Maryknoll, N.Y.: Orbis, 1973.

Phillips, D. Z. *Death and Immortality.* London: Macmillan, 1970.

Raboteau, Albert J. *Slave Religion.* New York: Oxford University Press, 1978.

Radcliffe-Brown, A. R. *The Andaman Islanders.* Glencoe, Ill.: Free Press, 1964.

———, and Daryl Forde, eds. *African Systems of Kinship and Marriage.* New York: Oxford University Press, 1950.

Ray, Benjamin C. *African Religions*. Englewood Cliffs, N.J.: Prentice-Hall, 1976.

Sangree, Walter H. "Youth as Elders and Infants as Ancestors: The Complementarity of Alternate Generations, Both Living and Dead in Tiriki, Kenya, and Irigwe, Nigeria," *Africa* 44, no. 1 (1974): 65–70.

Santandreas, S. "Evil and Witchcraft among the Ndogo Group of Tribes," *Africa* 11, no. 4 (1938): 459–81.

Sawyerr, Harry. *Creative Evangelism*. London: Lutterworth, 1968.

Sinda, Martial. *Le Messianisme congolais*. Paris: Payot, 1972.

Stanley, Henry Morton. *The Congo*. 2 vols. London: Sampson Low and Co., 1885.

Turner, Victor. *Revelation and Divination in Ndembu Ritual*. Ithaca, N.Y.: Cornell University Press, 1975.

Vincent, Thomas Louis. *La Mort africaine: Idéologie funéraire en Afrique noire*. Paris: Payot, 1982.

Wing, J. van. *Etudes Bakongo*. Bruges: Desclée de Brouwer, 1959.

INDEX

Afterdeath world: described by near-death returnees, 88–89, 93, 94–95; variety of spirits in, 136. *See also* Mpemba

Ancestors: active in daily affairs of the living, 90; source of chief's authority, 16; communication with, 17; source of communal blessings, 18; wisdom and guidance, 140; ritual for restoring harmony with, 18; as representing full humanness, 132, 134; as God's intermediaries, 132, 134; veneration of, 19, 133

Apparitions of the dead, 129, 136–37

Birth, initiation ceremony for the newborn, 32

Birthdays, celebrated communally, 37

Burial: rituals, 116–20; child burials, 123–24; desire for burial in own village, 117. *See also* Kifwidi (post-burial rite)

Chief. *See* Leadership

Christian churches: and persistence of traditional belief, ix, 29, 46, 78–82, 138–39, 140; role at funerals, 126–28; role in marriages, 28

Clan: defined, 11, 13, 14; responsibilities of members, 13–14

Communalism: vs. Western individualism, x; embodiment of spiritual reality, 1; as primary principle, 10; social mechanisms to preserve, 8–10; land ownership, 15; shaping of individuals, 32–35

Confession, ritual in syncretic churches, 76–77

Cousins, marriage between, 21

Curse: as expression of communal will, 30–31; use by ndoki, 84–85; from the dead upon the living, 115

Death: origin myths, 36–38, 134; attributed to kindoki, 40; attributed to spirits, 40; preparation for, 98–99; contamination of the living, 101–104; purification from, 120. *See also* Afterdeath world; Mpemba

Divorce, 29–30

Dreams: as communication from the dead, 77, 85, 97, 115, 117, 119; warning of impending death, 91

Education: value placed on, 4; and women, 7; to impart knowledge of tradition, 75; as cause of changing attitudes toward tradition, 99. *See also* Kinkimba

Evil: accepted as part of human nature, 46–47; defined as human oppression, 132

Evil dead, 131. *See also* Ndoki

Father, role in family, 20–21

Fetish, 67–68

Gender: division of responsibilities, 5–7, 23; and village layout, 5

Gifts: marriage, 21–25; funeral, 116

God: Kongo tradition vs. Christian, 1, 108; beyond definition, 135; as all-inclusive power, 137; as source of humanness and freedom, 132; and mythical origins of death, 36

Grandparents, role of, 22

Grave robbers (munziula), 52

Illness, as communal concern, 39

Immortality of spiritual bodies, 129

Independent churches. *See* Syncretic churches

Jesus: adaptation to Kongo tradition, 133; as ancestor, 139; as already present in African belief, 147n.2

SIMON BOCKIE was born in Banza-Lele village, Kivunda district, in the Manianga area of Lower Zaire. He majored in African religions and cultures at the University of Zaire and spent a year in Jerusalem, where he studied the Bible and modern Hebrew. He holds a Ph.D. in History and Phenomenology of Religion from the Graduate Theological Union.